Seeking Virtue

Seeking Virtue

Through History and Scripture

DAVID GOZA

WIPF & STOCK · Eugene, Oregon

SEEKING VIRTUE
Through History and Scripture

Copyright © 2020 David Goza. All rights reserved. Except for brief quotations in critical publications or reviews, no part of this book may be reproduced in any manner without prior written permission from the publisher. Write: Permissions, Wipf and Stock Publishers, 199 W. 8th Ave., Suite 3, Eugene, OR 97401.

Scripture is taken from the New King James Version®. Copyright © 1982 by Thomas Nelson. Used by permission. All rights reserved.

Wipf & Stock
An Imprint of Wipf and Stock Publishers
199 W. 8th Ave., Suite 3
Eugene, OR 97401

www.wipfandstock.com

PAPERBACK ISBN: 978-1-5326-9892-7
HARDCOVER ISBN: 978-1-5326-9893-4
EBOOK ISBN: 978-1-5326-9894-1

Manufactured in the U.S.A.   05/28/20

This book is dedicated to my family.
To my three boys: Nate, Alex, and Will.
To my beautiful daughter, Anna.
To my wife, Dana, without whom I would not be where I am today.

Contents

Acknowledgments	xi
Introduction	xiii
Guide to Ancient Sources	xv
Chapter 1: Virtues for Living Well	1
Generosity	2
Fortitude	5
Firm Heart	8
Diligence	10
Magnanimity	14
Humility	16
Contentment	18
Purity	20
Patience	22
Perseverance	23
Respect	25
Honesty	26
A Virtuous Lifestyle	26
Pursuing Virtue	29
Chapter 2: Facing Trials and Opposition	31
The Blessing of Trials	34
Times that Try Men's Souls	38
Remove Inimical Proceedings	41
Dealing with Wolves	43
Fighting Spiritual Battles	44
The Trial of Sickness	48
Good Judgment	50

CONTENTS

    An Occasion for Prayer …… 52

Chapter 3: Achieving Greatness …… 57
    Focus …… 58
    Pay the Price …… 59
    Sacrifice …… 64
    Self-confidence/Sense of Destiny …… 66
    Never Quit …… 67
    Submission …… 69
    Work Hard …… 71

Chapter 4: Things to Avoid …… 77
    Vices …… 77
    Blind Ignorance …… 81
    Burnout …… 82
    Envy …… 83
    Greed …… 85
    Disloyalty …… 87
    Pride …… 88
    Dwelling on the Past …… 93
    Lust …… 94
    An Uncontrolled Tongue …… 97
    Flattery …… 100
    Hypocrisy …… 101
    Drunkenness …… 102
    Mixed Up Priorities …… 105

Chapter 5: Things You Need …… 108
    Boldness …… 109
    Wisdom …… 111
    Discernment …… 119
    Integrity …… 121
    Knowledge …… 123
    Friendship …… 124
    Self-Restraint …… 129
    Love …… 130
    Peace …… 133

Chapter 6: Live with an Eternal Perspective	**144**
Life is Short	145
Beautiful In Its Time	149
Live Like You Are Dying	150
What You Really Own	151
The Race of Life	153
Conclusion	*156*
Bibliography	*157*
Subject Index	*161*

Acknowledgments

There are many people that I need to thank for helping bring this project together. First, I thank my wife, Dana, for her encouragement and proofreading. Without your help I would not have been able to complete this book. Thank you to my mother, for setting me on the course of faith and faithfully praying for me. Thank you to Dr. Boyd Luter, my father in law, for using his expertise in editing. I also would like to thank my assistant Kay McDaniel and my friend Dr. Chad Davis for assisting in proofreading the text.

Introduction

I have been asked numerous times, "What is your book about?" It is a question that I found difficult to answer in a specific way. This book is about "living well" and being inspired to live an honorable life through consideration of the lives of great men and women in history and the Bible. My original intent in writing this book was to put something into the hands of my four children that will inspire them to dream great dreams and to attempt great things in this world. I have always been inspired by reading classic works of history, and, of course, the Bible is the ultimate sourcebook for inspiration.

Reading history helps us in a number of ways. If there is something we need to change in our lives, we can learn it by observing others. Polybius says:

> For there are two ways by which all men can reform themselves, the one through their own mischances, the other through those of others, and of these the former is the more impressive, but the latter less hurtful.[1]

If we need to learn how to deal with the different circumstances of life:

> men have no more ready corrective of conduct than knowledge of the past. But all historians, one may say without exception, and in no half-hearted manner, but making this the beginning and end of their labour, have impressed on us that the soundest education and training for a life of active politics is the study of History, and that surest and indeed the only method of learning how to bear bravely the vicissitudes of fortune, is to recall the calamities of others.[2]

---

1. Polybius, *Histories*, Loc. 622–23.
2. Polybius, *Histories*, Loc. 80–83.

Introduction

By reading history, we can learn from the folly and misfortunes of others. We are sure to have our own, but it is good to know how those who went before dealt with them.

Polybius records a speech of Aemilius Paullus, who said:

> The difference between foolish and wise men lies in this, that the former are schooled by their own misfortunes and the latter by those of others.[3]

It is my hope that, when you read this book, you will be schooled by the misfortunes of others instead of your own and that you will be enlightened by the wisdom and successes of others, that you might achieve all that God has for you in life.

---

3. Polybius, *Histories*, Loc. 15531–39.

Guide to Ancient Sources

Herodotus: *The Landmark Herodotus: The Histories*

Herodotus was a Greek writer and considered the first historian. He wrote his famous history in the mid-fifth century BC. The work consists of an account of the Greek and Persian wars and his observations during his travels. Herodotus is especially important to Christians due to his descriptions of people and places mentioned in the Scriptures.

Thucydides: *The Landmark Thucydides: A Comprehensive Guide to the Peloponnesian War*

Thucydides (460–404 BC) is considered by many to be the greatest ancient Greek historian. He wrote a history of the Peloponnesian War, which recounts the struggle between Athens and Sparta in the fifth century BC. He was an eyewitness to many of the events that he wrote about, which makes his book all the more interesting.

Marcus Tullius Cicero: *Letters of Marcus Tullius Cicero with His Treatises on Friendship and Old Age*

Cicero (106–43 BC) was the greatest orator of the late Roman Republic. He was a famous lawyer and one of the leading political figures in the age of Julius Caesar. The "Letters" of Cicero provide us a fascinating look into the culture of Rome in the first century before Christ. His book "On Friendship" is an inspiring treatise on personal relationships.

Guide to Ancient Sources

Arrian: *The Landmark Arrian: The Campaigns of Alexander*

Arrian (AD 86–160) was a Roman citizen and held numerous prominent political positions. Arrian also served in the Roman military and held high commands in the army. His background provided him with the necessary knowledge to write a detailed account of the campaigns of Alexander the Great. Arrian's work is the most accurate and detailed account of Alexander to come from the ancient world.

Marcus Aurelius: *Meditations*

Marcus Aurelius (AD 121–180) was a Roman emperor. In addition to being one of the greatest Roman emperors, Aurelius was also a Stoic philosopher. The *Meditations* is a classic in Stoic philosophy and is an account of his personal reflections on life through the lens of Stoicism.

Epictetus: *The Discourses*

Epictetus was a Greek Stoic philosopher who lived during the reign of Nero (AD 54–68). He lived in Nicopolis, Greece, where he started a school called "healing place for sick souls." The works of Epictetus are very practical in nature and deal with ethical issues of everyday life.

Diogenes Laertius: *Lives of Eminent Philosophers*

Diogenes lived in the third century AD. He was a Greek Epicurean philosopher. His work on the lives of philosophers is a history of Greek philosophy. The value of the work is found in its extensive collection of quotations and facts.

Ammianus Marcellinus: *The Roman History of Ammianus Marcellinus*

Ammianus Marcellinus (AD 330–395) was born in Antioch, Syria, and died in Rome. He was born in a Greek family and served in the army of Constantius II. He was the last Roman historian and his history picked up where the history of Tacitus ended.

Valerius Maximus: *Memorable Deeds and Sayings: One Thousand Tales from Ancient Rome*

Maximus lived in the early first century; his history was written during the same years that Jesus was working and ministering in Israel. Maximus was a historian, but his book is mainly a collection of anecdotes from other historians. His purpose for the book was to illustrate virtues and vices in the lives of famous Greeks and Romans.

Pliny the Younger: *Letters of Gaius Plinius Caecilius Secundus*

Pliny (AD 62–115) was the son of the famous Roman scholar Pliny the Elder. Pliny the Younger was a Roman who served in the Senate and was governor of Bithynia. The "Letters" of Pliny are among the most important sources that have been preserved. Pliny wrote a series of letters to the Emperor Trajan where he described the persecution of Christians.

Plutarch: *Plutarch's Lives: The Lives of the Noble Grecians and Romans*

Plutarch (AD 45–120) was a Platonist philosopher and historian. He is best known as the author of "Parallel Lives." In this work Plutarch compared the lives of Greek and Roman leaders and generals. This work is one of the most important ancient sources and has inspired generations of readers.

Polybius: *The Complete Histories of Polybius*

Polybius (208–125 BC) was a Greek historian. The *Histories of Polybius* cover a time period which he personally witnessed. The work describes how the Roman Republic grew and dominated the ancient world. He also provided an eyewitness account of the sack of Carthage.

Suetonius: *The Lives of the Caesars*

Suetonius (AD 69–122) was a Roman biographer. His family was of the knightly class, which made him dependent on those from noble families. Suetonius became a friend of Pliny the Younger, who aided his literary career. His most famous work was a history of the Caesars in which he described the lives and scandals of the great Roman emperors, including Julius Caesar.

Tacitus: *The Annals of Imperial Rome*

Tacitus (AD 56–117) was one of the important historians of Roman antiquity. He was a friend of Pliny the Younger and member of the knightly class. In his most famous work, *The Annals*, Tacitus described the reigns of Tiberius, Claudius, and Nero. He is best known for his description of the cruel treatment of Christians at the hand of Nero. He was a contemporary of the apostle Paul and his history coincides with the years covered in the book of Acts.

Erasmus: *Collected Works of Erasmus.*

Desiderius Erasmus (1469–1536) lived in Basel, Switzerland. He was a great scholar and leader of the northern Renaissance. Erasmus is best known as the first editor of the New Testament. He was also an important figure in patristic and classical literature. He was one of the first to utilize the historical-critical study of the Greek New Testament and the writings of the church fathers.

Chapter 1

Virtues for Living Well

But also for this very reason, giving all diligence, add to your faith *virtue,* to virtue knowledge, to knowledge self-control, to self-control perseverance, to perseverance godliness, to godliness brotherly kindness, and to brotherly kindness love.

(2 Peter 1:5–7)[1]

If you look up the word "virtue" in a dictionary it says that the word means "moral excellence" or "righteousness." A virtue is a personal characteristic that causes one to be virtuous, to be moral or upright. In the ancient world, the pursuit of virtue was considered a noble and high calling. Ancient historians praised the virtues of statesmen, philosophers, and generals. They saw virtue as the greatest good for society and government.

Although most fell far short of a virtuous life, they still viewed it as an object to pursue and admired those who attained it. The great Greek leader Pericles argued that people who spend time on activities that are of little value just prove that they are negligent and lacking virtue. Wasting time just proves that you lack character. Pericles wrote:

---

1. Emphasis added in every epigraph to highlight the appearance of virtues in the passage.

> But virtue, by the bare statement of its actions, can so affect men's minds as to create at once both admiration of the things done and desire to imitate the doers of them.[2]

This statement by Pericles reveals the benefits of virtuous living. Instead of wasting valuable time doing things that do not improve yourself or society, those who live according to virtue will be admired by all and will be considered a leader among their peers. What follows in this chapter is a list of virtues that anyone would do well to study and apply to their life.

GENEROSITY

> Cast your bread upon the waters, For you will find it after many days.
> (Eccl 11:1)

In this verse, Solomon referred to something that people in his day would have understood immediately. To cast bread upon the waters was a way of speaking about engaging in commercial investments involving overseas trade. This was a common form of investment in the ancient world. Solomon knew all about overseas commercial trading.

Of course, investing in the ancient world, like today, was not without risks. If a businessman sent out his life savings in the form of grain on a ship that was to carry it across the Mediterranean Sea, there was a significant chance that he would never see it again. The ship could get lost, shipwrecked, or robbed by pirates. If all those things were avoided, it would be months before the ship would come back with the return on his investment; but when it did, the merchant's faith and patience would be rewarded.

Solomon used this as a metaphor for generosity. Give in faith, throw it on the waters, and God, who sees what you do in faith, will reward you and bring it back to you. Solomon is saying that, in all your investing, while you are doing business and hoping for a good return, do not neglect charity. Do not forget about the Lord "when your ship comes in." In the same way you throw your bread upon the waters in business, do the same thing by giving generously in faith and throwing it out on the waters.

Jesus promised in Luke 6:38, "Give and it will be given to you, good measure, pressed down, shaken together, and running over will be put into your bosom. For with the same measure that you use, it will be measured

2. Plutarch, *Lives*, 1:202.

back to you." Be generous in your giving. When you give in faith, it is a promise from God's word that he will return it to you. Your return may not necessarily be in the form of money, but it will be a form of blessing.

We need to realize that this is a characteristic of faith, and it will lead to generosity. We all know in business that you have to spend money to make money, and you have to invest in order to see a return. We sacrifice now, so that in the future we will have plenty. That is true in the business world, but it is also true in the spiritual world. Those who possess faith give generously, and God provides for their needs. Faith teaches us that what we sacrifice for Christ now does not compare with the riches and the glory we will have in the future.

In Ecclesiastes 11:2, Solomon said, "Give a serving to seven, and also to eight, for you do not know what evil will be on the earth." This is a Hebrew idiom. It was a way of saying to "just give, and God will abundantly bless it." Give freely to the poor, as that which is cast upon the waters. Send it on a voyage, and trust it upon the waters; it will not sink.

Give in faith, because Solomon added in the same verse, "For you do not know what evil will be on the earth." Many make use of this as an argument against giving to the poor or tithing to the church, because they do not know what hard times might await them in the future. Instead of giving a storehouse tithe, they choose to storehouse save.

We are tempted to think that we can protect ourselves by hoarding our money. It is foolishness; if we give in faith, when evil days come, we may have the comfort of having done good while we were able. We would then hope to find mercy both with God and man. By giving in faith we trust God with what we have; we put it into good hands against bad times. Do not become greedy and a hoarder; strive to live below your means and learn the joy of giving. I like how the old-time evangelist, Billy Sunday, said it:

> If you want to use your genius and ability to get all you can and use the surplus over your own needs for the good of humanity, I hope you all will be millionaires. If you want to get all you can, and can all you get, I hope you'll all go to the poorhouse.[3]

Faith leads to generosity not only in giving money. To be generous means to be unselfish. It is a virtue found in those who are not petty and small-minded. Generosity is a virtue that inspires admiration and can be very useful when confronting opposition. Polybius described it like this:

---

3. Sunday, "The Devil's Boomerangs," 225.

> And surely to conquer one's enemies by generosity and equity is of far higher service than any victory in the field; for to arms the vanquished yield from necessity, to virtue from conviction.[4]

Be generous with your money and time; this will lead to God's blessing on your life. Be generous in victory and even your enemies will praise you.

The virtue of generosity also influences how we treat others. When Alexander the Great marched across the world, he conquered not only with the aid of his powerful armies and military genius, but also with his generosity. The ancient historian Arrian recorded the occasion when Alexander led his armies all the way to India and fought a great battle against a powerful Indian king named Poros, whom he defeated:

> When Alexander learned that Poros was approaching, he met him in front of the line with a few of the Companions. Halting his horse, he marveled at Poros' height (which appeared to exceed eight feet), his beauty, and the fact that his spirit was plainly unbowed: he approached Alexander as one brave man would approach another, having contended honorably against another king on behalf of his kingdom. Alexander spoke first and urged Poros to say what he hoped would befall him. Poros is said to have replied, "Treat me like a king, Alexander." Pleased with the response, Alexander said, "That will be done, Poros, on my own account. But on your account, say what would be to your liking." Poros replied that everything was contained in that wish. And Alexander, even more pleased with this response, granted Poros sovereignty over the very Indians he had been ruling and added another territory even more extensive than his former domain. Thus he had treated a brave man like a king, and thereafter enjoyed the man's unswerving loyalty.[5]

The virtue of generosity is working in our lives when we can show generosity even to those who oppose us. The Scripture tells us to pray for our enemies; Jesus loved us even when we were his enemies. Alexander treated his enemy like a king, and this caused his enemy to become his loyal friend.

Being generous with your money is noble and good, but it is even better when you are generous in your actions to those who may be under your authority in some capacity. If a person has a lot of money, it is easy for them to be generous to those in need. However, if you find yourself competing

---

4. Polybius, *Histories*, Loc. 5469–70.
5. Arrian, *Campaigns of Alexander*, 220.

with someone for a position at work, or on a school sports team, and his or her failure is your advancement, it is a virtuous person who is generous to those who oppose them. One might say such a person is noble. It is an act of nobility to be generous to those who oppose you or those who are not your equal in some area of life. Plato once stated that this is the highest form of nobility:

> Nobility has four divisions. First, when the ancestors are gentle and handsome and also just, their descendants are said to be noble. Secondly, when the ancestors have been princes or magistrates, their descendants are said to be noble. The third kind arises when the ancestors have been illustrious; for instance, through having held military command or through success in the national games. For then we call the descendants noble. The last division includes the man who is himself of a generous and high-minded spirit. He too is said to be noble. And this indeed is the highest form of nobility. Thus, of nobility, one kind depends on excellent ancestors, another on princely ancestors, a third on illustrious ancestors, while the fourth is due to the individual's own beauty and worth.[6]

Some are considered noble because they were born into a great family, or they were born into money. But the highest nobility is found in a man or woman who is generous, for no other reason than it is in their heart to be kind and compassionate. This is the beautiful spirit of a generous heart, and it is a great virtue to possess.

FORTITUDE

> There is a natural firmness in some minds which cannot be unlocked by trifles, but which, when unlocked, discovers a cabinet of fortitude . . .[7] (Thomas Paine)

Fortitude is grit; it is strength of character. It is a virtue that shines through during times of stress. If you find yourself facing a difficult situation and you have no idea how you will overcome it, this is a virtue you will need. Those who possess fortitude will not cave under emotional or physical pressure. You might not overcome immediately, and you might get knocked down.

---

6. Diogenes, *Lives of Eminent Philosophers*, 355.
7. Paine, *Collected Writings*, 94.

Seeking Virtue

However, if you act with fortitude you will get up again and again until you win or die trying.

A person with fortitude is a person with a great heart. There is no desire for personal glory or a need to be the life of the party. Those who possess this virtue are calm and humble but at the same time passionate and trustworthy. This "cabinet of fortitude" is often discovered in the most unexpected places.

In 1 Samuel 16, the prophet Samuel was directed by God to go to Bethlehem and anoint one of the sons of Jesse to be king. The seven sons of Jesse were paraded before Samuel and he did what most people would do: he looked at their outward characteristics and assumed that God's anointed would be someone extraordinary to look upon.

That is how we do things when we are living in the flesh, and our minds are focused on the world. We look at outward characteristics. If a person is beautiful and charismatic, gives a good interview, or knows how to carry themselves, we are drawn to them. When Samuel laid eyes on Eliab, the oldest son, he said, "Surely the Lord's anointed is before him." Surely this is the one; he is tall, dark, and handsome. Samuel was ready to settle on Eliab until God rebuked him.

Is it not strange that Samuel the prophet was ready to settle for someone who was just like the wicked king Saul? He said surely this is the one. But he was not the one. And then God revealed something new and told Samuel, "Do not look at his appearance or at his physical stature, because I have refused him. For the Lord does not see as man sees, for man looks at the outward appearance, but the Lord looks at the heart" (1 Sam 16:7).

And that is the truth of God; he does not look merely at the outside of a man, but on the inside. God saw in the heart of David a "cabinet of fortitude." As Paul wrote in 1 Corinthians 1:27–29, "But God has chosen the foolish things of the world to put to shame the wise, and God has chosen the weak things of the world to put to shame the things which are mighty; and the base things of the world and things which are despised God has chosen . . . to bring to nothing the things that are, that no flesh should glory in his presence."

In our flesh, we are tempted to look on the outside characteristics of people and assume that because they are attractive, gifted, or tall they are the most qualified. And we are disappointed as time goes by because of their lack of spiritual depth and commitment. But, when God chooses someone, he chooses a person who has a heart of faith.

We know from the Scripture that not many mighty or noble are called to serve the Lord. God loves using the weak and untrained, like the uneducated fishermen of Galilee, to do his will. In this way God alone gets the glory. The Scripture says in 2 Chronicles 16:9, "For the eyes of the Lord run to and fro throughout the whole earth, to show Himself strong on behalf of those whose heart is loyal to Him." And I believe God is especially interested in setting people apart when they are young, as he did when he called David to be king. He looks into our inner being and knows our potential. Never underestimate a youth just based on outward appearances or behavior, for you never know what is in their heart.

Plutarch shared the story of Fabius as an example of this virtue:

> Our Fabius, who was fourth in descent from that Fabius Rullus who first brought the honourable surname of Maximus into his family, was also, by way of personal nickname, called Verrucosus, from a wart on his upper lip; and in his childhood they in like manner named him Ovicula, or The Lamb, on account of his extreme mildness of temper. His slowness in speaking, his long labour and pains in learning, his deliberation in entering into the sports of other children, his easy submission to everybody, as if he had no will of his own, made those who judge superficially of him, the greater number, esteem him insensible and stupid; and few only saw that this tardiness proceeded from stability, and discerned the greatness of his mind, and the lionlikeness of his temper. But as soon as he came into employments, his virtues exerted and showed themselves; his reputed want of energy then was recognised by people in general as a freedom of passion; his slowness in words and actions, the effect of a true prudence; his want of rapidity and his sluggishness, as constancy and firmness.[8]

The example of Fabius shows that we must be careful about making judgments about people without first seeing how they respond to adversity. Sometimes those who are the most meek and mild in everyday life show themselves during times of adversity to have a heart like a lion.

The virtue of fortitude is different than aggressiveness or strength or even passion. Fortitude is a virtue that can be found in the most mild-mannered person. Christians are to be like Christ in this way: Jesus was as gentle as a lamb, but in his heart were strength and fortitude.

People in the world may make superficial and surface-level judgments about us. The world judges by what they see on the outside, but God looks

---

8. Plutarch, *Lives*, 2:235.

on the inside of a man. In your heart cultivate this virtue of fortitude. It will strengthen you against the false judgments of others, and it will serve you well in times of adversity. Superficial, shallow-hearted people wilt under the pressure of opposition. But the heart of fortitude faces adversity with patience and unyielding confidence.

FIRM HEART

> But Daniel *purposed in his heart* that he would not defile himself with the portion of the king's delicacies, nor with the wine which he drank; therefore he requested of the chief of the eunuchs that he might not defile himself.
> (Dan 1:8)

> Shadrach, Meshach, and Abed-Nego answered and said to the king, "O Nebuchadnezzar, we have no need to answer you in this matter. If that is the case, our God whom we serve is able to deliver us from the burning fiery furnace, and He will deliver us from your hand, O king. But if not, let it be known to you, O king, that we do not serve your gods, nor will we worship the gold image which you have set up."
> (Dan 3:16–18)

Daniel and his three friends demonstrated what a firm heart looks like. It is a heart that is resolved to do right, even if it means getting killed for it.

The world of Daniel and his three young friends was turned upside down when Nebuchadnezzar took them into captivity. Nebuchadnezzar, the king of Babylon, took captive the best and brightest of Judah. His plan was to gather the brightest young minds of the Jews and bring them into the Babylonian culture to serve him. He wanted to reeducate and retrain them and fill their minds with the philosophies of Babylon, including Babylonian science, astrology, and religion. His goal was to uproot their beliefs and traditional values.

Imagine the influence these pagan Babylonian teachers had on these Jewish teenagers. The Babylonians' literature promoted their worldview, their view of man, God, sin, and redemption, which were all directly opposed to everything these young teens had been taught in Israel. There was a tremendous amount of pressure and temptation for these boys to conform.

Nebuchadnezzar desired to assimilate them into Babylonian culture; to do this he tried to win their hearts and loyalty by pleasing their flesh. The attempt was to wipe out every memory of the God of their fathers through the king's delicacies (i.e., a royal life of plenty and luxury) and education. They were elevated far above the people. They were to enjoy a life fit for a king. Receiving royal treatment like this would be a big temptation to anyone. These youth were being tempted with the best the world had to offer, and they had to make a choice to either reject their God or stay faithful and refuse to be corrupted.

What would you do? Parents, how would your teenager fare under these circumstances? Would they give in to worldly pleasure? It was a great party scene, with wine and women and plenty of food.

What would you do? Would you compromise or would you remember the Lord? When you are surrounded by worldly people who are living in a way contrary to what God would have for you, there is going to be great pressure. And that is where most of us live day in and day out. That is why church is so important. You are to raise your family in the church, enmeshing your life in the life of the church, surrounding yourself with fellow believers who can help you overcome the world. The Scripture says Daniel "purposed in his heart." Daniel was resolved to follow God's word and not live like the world. He refused to compromise.

How does this relate to us in the current culture? We will find an element of relevance because, as Solomon proclaimed in Ecclesiastes, "there is nothing new under the sun." As Christians, we are living in what could be described as spiritual Babylon. God has called us and separated us; his will is for us to be different from the world and to not conform to the world's standards.

The world tries to make God's people conform to its belief system, which is always contrary to God's word. When God's people are in Babylon, they need to take special care that they "partake not in her sins."

Note this about Daniel: he was more afraid to commit sin than he was to disappoint a king. He was more fearful of the consequences of sin than he was of any outward trouble. Thomas Paine, a leader during the Revolutionary War, once wrote:

> I love the man that can smile in trouble, that can gather strength from distress, and grow brave by reflection. Tis the business of little

minds to shrink; but he whose heart is firm, and whose conscience approves his conduct, will pursue his principles unto death.[9]

A firm heart is a virtue that is seen when someone chooses to take a stand for what is right when everyone else is telling them to compromise. Consider the example of the American hero Davy Crockett. He was a champion for common people and despised elitism. Crockett was a Congressman in his second term when Andrew Jackson became president. Crockett initially endorsed his fellow Tennessean, but later they parted ways over the president's Indian Removal Act. Crockett was convinced it was unjust, which later proved to be truth, leading to the Trail of Tears. Accordingly, Crockett wrote:

> Several of my colleagues got around me, and told me how well they loved me, and that I was ruining myself. They said this was a favorite measure of the president, and I ought to go for it. I told them I believed it was a wicked, unjust measure, and that I should go against it, let the cost to myself be what it might.[10]

Davy Crockett was a man with a firm heart who decided to follow his convictions rather than the crowd. His strong moral stance cost him; he lost his next election because his constituents favored the bill. Crockett lost his job in Congress, but he established his legacy.

DILIGENCE

> "The soul of a lazy man desires, and has nothing; But the soul of the *diligent* shall be made rich."
> (Prov 13:4)

> "Therefore, brethren, be even more *diligent* to make your call and election sure, for if you do these things you will never stumble."
> (2 Pet 1:10)

Benjamin Franklin was known for his diligence when he was a young man and just starting out in business. It was not only his intellect that brought him fame and fortune, but it was the virtue of diligence that set him apart. In his autobiography, Franklin described his attitude and work ethic:

---

9. Paine, *Collected Writings*, 97.
10. Edmondson, *Alamo Story*, 271.

> This library afforded me the means of improvement by constant study, for which I set apart an hour or two each day, and thus repair'd in some degree the loss of the learned education my father once intended for me. Reading was the only amusement I allow'd myself. I spend no time in taverns, games, or frolicks of any kind; and my industry in my business continu'd as indefatigable as it was necessary. I was indebted for my printing-house; I had a young family coming on to be educated, and I had to contend with for business, two printers who were established in the place before me. My circumstances, however, grew daily easier. My original habits of frugality continuing, and my father having, among his instructions to me when a boy, frequently repeated a proverb of Solomon: "Seest thou a man diligent in his calling, he shall stand before kings, he shall not stand before mean men." [11]

The virtue of diligence will set you apart, and it will cause others to respect and trust you. When you are diligent in your calling, it means you will be motivated to cut out of your life those things that would distract you.

When one considers that time is a finite resource, those who are diligent will refuse to waste that precious resource on things outside of their calling. Those who succeed in their calling are those who work harder than their competitors, and this is true in any area of life, from ministry to even baseball.

Perhaps the greatest hitter of all time in major league baseball was Ted Williams. Most baseball fans know this, but most do not know the price paid by Williams to earn that title. His biographer, Ben Bradlee, described Williams this way:

> The self-made, intellectually curious Williams was ahead of his time in regarding hitting as a science worthy of study, experimentation, and technical analysis. He coddled the blunt instruments of his success: his bats. He boned them. He cleaned them with alcohol every night. He weighed them meticulously on small scales to make sure they hadn't gotten slightly heavier through condensation. And, acting on the improbable suggestion of a teenage boy from Chelsea, Massachusetts, he even heated his bats to keep their moisture content low.[12]

---

11. Franklin, *Autobiography*, 181.
12. Bradlee, *Ted Williams*, 16.

Williams always believed there was only one way to really be great: through hard work and practice. Williams once said:

> I would never have gained a headline for hitting if I hadn't kept everlastingly at it, and thought of nothing else the year round.[13]

Williams is a classic example of diligence and the power of this virtue to make a person great. No matter what calling God has placed on your life, your full potential will not be realized unless you pursue diligence as a virtue.

Paul said in 2 Timothy 2:15, "Be diligent to present yourself approved to God, a worker who does not need to be ashamed, rightly dividing the word of truth." Paul instructed us to rightly divide God's word, and that means we are to take care to understand it accurately.

How do we do this? By being diligent and working at studying God's word. It is a fact of life that those who work hard and practice diligence in whatever they do are the ones who will ultimately come out on top. Working hard coupled with a positive attitude and an inner drive leads to advancement. When we work hard and put in an honest day's work, it brings us fulfillment. It makes us happy and pleasant to be around.

On the other hand, when we are lazy or just do the minimum to get by, what happens? We get bored and say, "I do not have anything to do; my job is boring." When people fail to work hard, it leads to a host of other problems. This is human nature. One of the great observers of human nature was Benjamin Franklin. In his autobiography, Franklin recorded his experience as it related to human nature and work ethic. While on an expedition with the army in uncharted territory, they found an ideal location to build a fort. As Franklin explained:

> The next morning our fort was planned and marked out, our fort stockade, was finished in a week, though it rained so hard every other day the men could not work. This gave me occasion to observe that, when men are employed, they are best contented; for on the days they worked they were good-natured and cheerful and, with the consciousness of having done a good day's work, they spent the evening jollily; but on our idle days they were mutinous and quarrelsome, finding fault with their pork, the bread, etc., and in continual ill-humor, which put me in mind of a sea-captain, whose rule it was to keep his men constantly at work, and, when his mate once told him that they had done every thing, and there

---

13. Bradlee, *Ted Williams*, 41.

was nothing further to employ them about, "*Oh*," says he, "*make them scour the anchor.*"[14]

To "scour the anchor" meant that the men were to take hard, coarse brushes and scrub and clean the anchor. Yes, it was busy work, but it was also necessary work. The anchor for a ship is vital and is what enables the ship to settle, to keep from drifting, to protect the vessel from being run aground and tossed around by the wind and waves. Scouring the anchor was the nitty gritty, fundamental necessity of caring for the ship.

There is always work to be done. When people are lazy and feel there is nothing to do, it leads to unhappiness; idleness leads to fighting and bickering. What is true in the business world is also true in the spiritual world. There are times in our spiritual life that all the other work is done; we need to scour the anchor spiritually.

The worst thing that we can do spiritually is to sit idly by and get bored. One can look at some people and discern that their faith and the Bible has little effect on their life. There is no excitement in their spiritual life. They are not using their spiritual gifts or improving their walk with the Lord. They say, "I do not know what to do." Just like the sea captain said to his crew, if you do not know what to do, then scour your spiritual anchor. Get back to the basics.

What is the spiritual anchor of the Christian? The "word of truth." God's word is the anchor of the church and of our individual lives. It is that which keeps us from drifting; it anchors us so that the winds and waves of life do not take us for a ride.

Reading God's word is fundamental for our spiritual health. Though it takes hard work, sometimes even though we do not feel like it, we need to take up our anchor and scour it. We have to use our spiritual muscles; we have to get in it with some elbow grease and grind into the word of God. That is scouring our spiritual anchor. There is never a time in our spiritual life that we should ever be bored and feel like we have nothing to do. The spiritual anchor is always there and it always needs our attention. But it requires hard work. Paul says to "be diligent." This word literally means "do your best," "be zealous or eager," "make every effort." Be diligent as Paul encouraged in 2 Timothy 2:15: "Be diligent to present yourself approved to God, a worker who does not need to be ashamed."

---

14. Franklin, *Autobiography*, 277.

Seeking Virtue

MAGNANIMITY

> "I shall be next to you..."
> (1 Sam 23:27)

These words in 1 Samuel were spoken by Jonathan to his rival for the throne, David. Jonathan loved David and, in a great act of magnanimity, willingly took second place so that David could become king of Israel.

I love the word "magnanimous"! The word "magnanimous" is a combination of two Latin words: *magnus* (great) and *animus* (spirit). It means to be bighearted. A magnanimous person is able to face trouble calmly, to set aside revenge, and to make sacrifices of personal desires for the sake of the greater good. It is the opposite of pride and jealousy.

To be magnanimous means to be generous, especially when wronged. A magnanimous spirit causes one to sacrifice self for the greater good.

It was the virtue of magnanimity that helped lift Abraham Lincoln out of obscurity to become the president of the United States. A few years before his election, "Lincoln for President" seemed out of the question. In May of 1856, he went to the Illinois Legislature as a candidate for senator, and when the ballots were cast, Lincoln was only four shy of being elected. But one of his opponents, Trumbull, led a small coalition of five and refused to drop out and give his few votes to Lincoln. Both Lincoln and his opponent were on the same side politically and were running on an anti-slavery platform. After nine ballots, Lincoln knew that, unless he or his opponent gave up their votes, a pro-slavery candidate would be elected. Lincoln was unwilling to let this happen, and he removed his name from the ballot. All of Lincoln's supporters with regret switched their votes, giving Trumbull the win.

Lincoln expressed no hard feelings toward Trumbull and even attended his victory party, saying that he was glad that their opponents were beaten. Lincoln's supporters believed this was his last chance for high office. But Lincoln's magnanimity on this occasion had an unexpected effect, as it earned him more respect and fame than he would have otherwise received in victory. Not knowing this at the time, the men he would be running against for president in 1860 had all made political enemies in their victories. At the same time Lincoln, being gracious in defeat, gained much love and respect, which eventually would lead to his election as president. Lincoln once said:

Virtues for Living Well

I am slow to listen to criminations among friends, and never expouse their quarrels on either side . . . allow by-gones to be by-gones, and look to the present & future only.[15]

Lincoln was magnanimous in defeat. He surrendered his personal ambitions for the sake of unity because he believed in the cause more than he desired personal glory.

Strive to cultivate a magnanimous spirit. Jesus tells us to pray and to do good to those who use us and treat us spitefully. When we act with the virtue of magnanimity, it will produce the fruit of friendship and inspire the admiration of others.

In Scripture, there are numerous examples of this virtue. None is greater perhaps than Abraham in Genesis 13. In this chapter, Abraham was in a land dispute with his nephew Lot. Lot's servants were in constant strife with the servants of Abraham. Both houses had grown great and there was not enough pasture left between the two, and now the strife was threatening to affect the relationship between Abraham and Lot.

Abraham had a magnanimous spirit. He could have said, "Hey now, wait a minute, I am your uncle; not only that, but I am the chosen one, and God has given me this land." But Abraham would have gained nothing by this; the land was promised to his descendants, and it did not matter where his cows grazed.

Abraham had nothing to gain by pridefully digging in his heals against Lot, but he had everything to gain by being magnanimous. Abraham went to his nephew and told him to choose between Caanan and the Jordan Valley. In effect, Abraham was offering the promised land to Lot. God had said in Genesis 12:7, "To your descendants I will give this land," and therefore Abraham knew that even if he gave the land away a thousand times, it would still go to his descendants.

Even though Abraham had the right to choose his land and was older and more wealthy than Lot, for the sake of peace and brotherly love he told Lot to choose which part of the land he wanted. Abraham said, "If you go to the right, I will go to the left." That is a magnanimous spirit.

Can you imagine Lot's reaction? I am sure when Abraham called the meeting Lot arrived filled with pride and ready to be on the defensive, but when Abraham gave him the choice, he had nothing to say but "Thanks."

Great leaders are "great" at showing kindness to those who work for them. A magnanimous spirit is necessary for a public figure and leader. The

---

15. Goodwin, *Team of Rivals*, 272.

famous Greek leader Pericles had his ups and downs in his public service. He devoted his life to serving the people of Athens. Everything he did was in their service. Sometimes they loved him, but sometimes they hated him. Plutarch recorded this story:

> Once, after being reviled and ill-spoken of all day long in his own hearing by some vile and abandoned fellow in the open marketplace, where he was engaged in the dispatch of some urgent affair, he continued his business in perfect silence, and in the evening returned home composedly, the man still dogging him at the heels, and pelting him all the way with abuse and foul language; and stepping into his house, it being by this time, dark, he ordered one of his servants to take a light, and to go along with the man and see him safely home.[16]

That is a magnanimous spirit. Such a spirit will always serve you well.

HUMILITY

> Likewise you younger people, submit yourselves to your elders. Yes, all of you be submissive to one another, and be clothed with *humility*, for "God resists the proud, But gives grace to the humble." (1 Pet 5:5)

Humility is one of the most important virtues that can be acquired. If you will not humble yourself, you will usually be humbled. Mark Twain was traveling with his brother to California and on the way they visited Salt Lake City. While there, he had the opportunity to meet with the ruler of the Mormon church. The following will explain how a young Mark Twain learned humility at the hand of Mormon leader Brigham Young:

> The second day, we made the acquaintance of Mr. Street and put on white shirts and went and paid a state visit to the king (Brigham Young). He seemed a quiet, kindly, easy-mannered, dignified, self-possessed old gentleman of fifty-five or sixty, and had a gentle craft in his eye that probably belonged there. He was very simply dressed and was just taking off a straw hat as we entered. He talked about Utah, and the Indians, and Nevada, and general American matters and questions, with our secretary and certain government officials who came with us. But he never paid any attention to me, notwithstanding I made several attempts to "draw him out" on

---

16. Plutarch, *Lives*, 2:606.

federal politics and his high-handed attitude toward Congress. I thought some of the things I said were rather fine. But he merely looked around at me, at distant intervals, something as I have seen a benignant old cat look around to see which kitten was meddling with her tail. By and by I subsided into an indignant silence, and so sat until the end, hot and flushed, and execrating him in my heart for an ignorant savage. But he was calm. His conversation with those gentlemen flowed on as sweetly and peacefully and musically as any summer brook. When the audience was ended and we were retiring from the presence, he put his hand on my head, beamed down on me in an admiring way and said to my brother: "Ah—your child, I presume? Boy, or girl?"[17]

A humble man or woman is one who does not think too highly of themselves. They think highly of God, but they reduce their own self-importance. A man who is proud and lifted up forgets that he is made of the dust of the ground. And in his spirit, being full of pride, he lifts himself up.

It is so easy for us to be proud and to magnify our own self-importance. When that happens, our pride causes us to overreact every time we perceive someone has slighted us. You know it is pride that is driving you when you are willing to hold on to bitterness and to cause division when you are upset about something small.

Compare what you are upset about to the injustices of this world; what is that little slight in light of a parent who loses a young child to an illness or tragedy? It is easy for us to offend God when we overreact to some small thing because of our arrogance.

How much better it is to be of a humble spirit with the lowly; it causes us to be pleasing in his sight. It is a beautiful thing to see a man or woman who is truly humble, because they look at themselves as they should, as clay in the potter's hand or as the dust of the ground. The humble person can watch others receive praise and glory without a spirit of jealousy and rejoice with others when good things happen to them. God dwells in the heart of a humble and contrite person. It is far better to clothe yourself with humility than having someone else do it for you. Humility is a virtue that God honors, but he resists the proud.

---

17. Twain, *Innocents Abroad*, 606.

CONTENTMENT

> Not that I speak in regard to need, for I have learned in whatever state I am, to be *content*: I know how to be abased, and I know how to abound. Everywhere and in all things I have learned both to be full and to be hungry, both to abound and to suffer need. I can do all things through Christ who strengthens me.
> (Phil 4:11–13)

A state of contentment is not to be confused with a lack of motivation or an absence of ambition. Contentment is ambition rightly directed. It is a virtue because it is a state of being and thinking that produces a healthy balance to life.

A person who is not content with their present circumstances is one who constantly worries over inconsequential matters. Difficult circumstances are common to all mankind, and worrying about them will not change a thing. A man or woman who has learned to be content is able to face adversity with peace in his or her heart. Such contentment causes us to be effective in serving others and making a positive contribution to our churches and society. But if we are discontent others view us as selfish; this severely affects our ability to be a positive influence on others.

Solomon said in Ecclesiastes 4:6: "Better a handful with quietness than both hands full, together with toil and grasping for the wind." In other words, it is better to be content with what you have than to spend life in the rat race filled with stress and anxiety to gain something that you cannot enjoy but for a short time. Those who are content live below their means and require nothing material to motivate them. They are the best leaders and have the greatest successes. But envy and greed destroy our effectiveness. One of the Roman emperors in *Plutarch's Lives* said this:

> For he has no time for great matters who concerns himself with petty ones; nor can he relieve many needs of others, who himself has many needs of his own. What most of all enables a man to serve the public is not wealth, but content and independence; which, requiring no superfluity at home, distracts not the mind from the common good. God alone is entirely exempt from all want: of human virtues, that which needs least is the most absolute and most divine.[18]

---

18. Plutarch, *Lives*, 2:482.

Those who are the most like Christ are those who need the least of the material things in this world. Jesus did not have a place to lay his head in this world, yet he was one with God the Father. Those who need the least are the most divine. If we spend our days constantly worried about little petty things, we will have no time to do great things for the Lord.

The Scripture says that we are to be content in all things. Let us strive to need very little that this world has to offer. Those who are filled with God's Spirit and focused on building up treasure in heaven will find themselves among those who need the least.

Cato of Tusculum, who was famous for his pure and temperate way of life, said with profound wisdom:

> When there is great care about food, there is very little care about virtue.[19]

Consider this quote from British Lieutenant William Digby, written in the midst of the American Revolution:

> ... but alas! This life is a constant rotation of changes; and the man, who forms the smallest hopes, has generally the greatest chance of happiness.[20]

Do not put your hope in the things of this world, but be heavenly minded. The things of this world are always changing hands; if you want to be truly happy, learn to be content. We are most content when our personal ambitions are aligned with the purposes of God's kingdom. When our desires are for bringing God glory and our greatest hopes are in what will be ours in heaven, contentment will be the result.

Let your hopes and ambitions in this world be small and your hope for heaven be great. This is the true meaning of contentment. Being content is a virtue, and it will protect you from selfish ambition and envy. You can be ambitious without being selfish in your ambition. Be ambitious to serve God, be ambitious to help others, but avoid the ambition to be praised by others. Plutarch summed it up like this:

> ... yet he who does not so much as desire others' praises, seems to me more perfectly virtuous, than he who is always extolling himself. A mind free from ambition is a main help to political

---

19. Marcellinus, *Roman History*, Loc. 1387–90
20. Digby, *Journal*, 309.

gentleness; ambition, on the contrary, is hard-hearted, and the greatest fomenter of envy.[21]

Strive to be ambitious about things that will glorify God. Learn to be content where you are and with what you have. Personal ambition for material possessions and social position will lead to envy in your heart.

PURITY

> Blessed are the *pure* in heart, for they shall see God.
> (Matt 5:8)

Whenever we think about purity, the first thing that comes to mind is activities of our physical bodies. When a Christian engages in sexual immorality, it is classified in Scripture as a grievous sin because our bodies are temples of the Holy Spirit. God expects Christians to save themselves for marriage. We are to be pure, but the purity of this beatitude goes even further than the physical; Jesus says blessed are the pure in heart.

The purity of the sixth beatitude means a heart that does not bring mixed motives and divided loyalties into its relationship with God. It is a heart of singleness in devotion to God—pure, unmixed devotion and pure motivations. James referred to this idea when he said, "Purify your hearts, you double-minded" (Jas 4:8). What we think, what we speak, and the things we do reveal the purity or the impurity of our hearts.

In the Bible, "heart" means more than just the mind; it also includes the emotions and the will. It refers to our ability to think, feel, and decide. Therefore, "pure in heart" means that not only our minds but also our feelings and actions are to be acceptable to God.

The heart refers to our will. It is that special place in the innermost part of our beings where we think and feel; it is that place from where our choices and decisions flow out. That innermost place is to be sanctified before God and devoted to him. We have to guard it daily because it is from the heart where all of our problems come as well. Jesus said in Matthew 15:19, "For out of the heart proceed evil thoughts, murders, adulteries, fornications, thefts, false witness, blasphemies."

In this world, someone might do what is right on the outside, but on the inside, in the heart, his or her reason for doing what is right is not pure.

---

21. Plutarch, *Lives*, 2:483.

It is bad enough if we sin in the flesh, but it is even worse when all of our sin is hidden from the sight of man. The sins of the heart are invisible to others, but they are constantly visible to God.

Some of us are professionals at hiding our sin from others and, as a result, we are in slavery to sin. It is easy to repent of sins done in public, but secret sins are more dangerous because we do not want anyone to know, so they enslave us. Jesus said that the pure in heart will see God. Those who have been purified by Christ and who daily walk in sanctification by prayer and confession and repentance see God, not in person but in their circumstances. The pure in heart see God when they go through a trial; they see the purpose behind the trial.

Joseph was almost killed by his brothers and then sold into slavery in Egypt. But God was faithful to Joseph through it all and blessed Joseph through his trials. Joseph was able to say to his brothers in Genesis 45:8, "It was not you who sent me here but God." Joseph had a pure heart.

Impurity of heart is the cause of spiritual blindness. To an impure heart, God cannot be seen anywhere; all they see are their troubles and what is right before them. They feel hopeless and depressed, but to a pure heart God is seen everywhere. "Blessed are the pure in heart." Strive to be pure not only in your hearts and thoughts but also in your motivations.

Herodotus provided us a great example of what pure motivations look like. A group of Arcadians had come to the king of Persia for help in finding employment. The king asked them about the Hellenes. The Hellenes referred to the Greek nation, which also included Arcadia. Herodotus recorded:

> The Arcadians told them that the Hellenes were celebrating the Olympic festival and watching an athletic competition and an equestrian contest. When he asked what prize they were competing for, they told him that the winner would receive an olive wreath. At that, Tritantaichmes son of Artabanos expressed a most noble insight which, however, made the King consider him a coward from that day on, for when he heard that their prize was an olive wreath rather than money, he could not bear to keep quiet, but cried out to them all, "Good grief, Mardonios, what kind of men did you lead us here to fight, who compete not for money but for excellence alone?"[22]

---

22. Herodotus, *Histories*, 611.

The Persians could not comprehend men competing in the Olympic festival without the motivation of financial reward. As soon as Tritantaichmes uttered those words, he revealed his heart to the king. From that point on, the king knew that this man served him with impure motives: for money.

Purity in motive is just as important as purity in your physical body. If you only compete or work for money, in the end you will be dissatisfied and others will deem you to be without character. Working or competing for money is not a pure motivation. The virtue of purity is seen most clearly in one who works or competes out of a love for the work or the competition. In everything you do, including your work and in sports, work as unto the Lord. Strive for excellence, not material gain. Jesus says that you should seek first his kingdom and righteousness, and he will add everything else that you need.

PATIENCE

> By your *patience* possess your souls.
> (Luke 21:19)

When General Ulysses S. Grant was promoted to supreme commander over the Union Army, he had many ambitious young men who desired to be promoted. In his autobiography, he made the following observation:

> It is men who wait to be selected, and not those who seek, from whom we may always expect the most efficient service.[23]

The virtue of patience is produced through faith and trust in the provision of the Lord. The Christian is not to seek self-promotion over others, but to put others first. This is the opposite of how the world thinks, but it is the pathway to true success for the Christian. By patience, we trust the Lord to promote us according to his will. It is for the Christian to serve the Lord faithfully wherever they are placed, always remembering the promise of God's word. If we are faithful in the small things, God will see to it that bigger things will come our way.

Patience is also produced through trials. The word "patience" literally means "bearing up under." God uses trials to produce this virtue in our

---

23. Grant, *Memoirs*, vi.

lives. This understanding of patience implies steadfastness, endurance, and fortitude.

One key way to acquire the virtue of patience is through the teacher of trials. Trials produce that quality within us. Every time a trial is overcome, we grow more confident that we can do it again. And the next time we find ourselves in the throes of a difficult circumstance, we will remember how the Lord delivered us, and we will have that confident expectation that he will do it again.

This was the experience of David when he saw the mammoth Philistine Goliath blaspheming God and embarrassing the armies of God. David was angered and, though just a young man, he approached King Saul and said, "Your servant will go and fight with this Philistine" (1 Sam 17:32).

Saul discouraged David by saying that he could not fight him because he was a youth, and Goliath was a man of war since his youth. Saul looked upon the small and ruddy shepherd boy and thought he was going to be easily crushed by the nine-foot-tall giant.

Do you remember what David said in response? David told him about the time he was out in the fields and a great bear came and snatched one of his sheep. God strengthened him to catch the bear by the beard and kill it with his bare hands. It was through a trial that David learned to keep the word of God and to use the virtue of patience when facing trials. David said in Psalm 119:67, "Before I was afflicted I went astray, but now I keep your Word."

This is the secret of the Christian life. It was a secret learned by Job; he said, "When he has tried me, I shall come forth as gold" (Job 23:10).

God always has a purpose for everything. God uses every trial and circumstance to produce a faith that is pure gold in his eyes. It is because we know the reasons and purposes of trials that we are able to exercise the attitude of joy while going through them. God uses trials to purify us, to produce patience within us, and to produce perfection in our faith.

PERSEVERANCE

> Tribulation produces *perseverance*, and perseverance, character . . .
> (Rom 5:3–4)

The Roman Republic was in the midst of a civil war when Sertorius, a Roman statesman and general stationed in Spain, began to lead a feeble army against the powerful legions of Rome. After winning a few key battles and establishing a strong government, the people and soldiers wanted Sertorius to lead them to attack and defeat the entire Roman army which opposed them.

Sertorius was smart and knew that they would be defeated if they attempted such a battle. He attempted to convince them to be patient and explained to them the need for caution and that they would defeat the Romans a little at a time. But the soldiers grew impatient with Sertorius. He then decided to let the most vocal lead a portion of the army and fight with the Romans. Sertorius knew they would be defeated, and he developed a plan to rescue them before they were utterly routed.

After the lessons learned from this battle, the soldiers were more obedient to his commands. After a few days Sertorius desired to encourage his soldiers after the recent defeat. Plutarch described how Sertorius convinced them to fight with perseverance rather than rash desperation:

> He had called all his army together, he caused two horses to be brought into the field, one old, feeble, lean animal, the other a lusty, strong horse, with a remarkably thick and long tail. Near the lean one he placed a tall, strong man, and near the strong young horse a weak, despicable-looking fellow; and at a sign given, the strong man took hold of the weak horse's tail with both his hands, and drew it to him with his whole force, as if he would pull it off; the other, the weak man, in the meantime, set to work to pluck off hair by hair from the great horse's tail. When the strong man had given trouble enough to himself in vain, and sufficient diversion to the company, and had abandoned his attempt, whilst the weak, pitiful fellow in a short time and with little pains had left not a hair on the great horse's tail, Sertorius rose up and spoke to his army. "You see, fellow-soldiers, that perseverance is more prevailing than violence, and that many things which cannot be overcome when they are together, yield themselves up when taken little by little. Assiduity and persistence are irresistible, and in time overthrow and destroy the greatest powers whatever."[24]

There are going to be challenges in life which will appear to be impossible to overcome. When you find yourself in such a circumstance, embrace the virtue of perseverance.

Fight the battles a little at a time, and avoid being rash and foolish.

---

24. Plutarch, *Lives*, 1:12–13.

RESPECT

> Honor all people. Love the brotherhood. Fear God. Honor the king.
> (1 Pet 2:17)

To honor all people means to respect them. The Christian is not to dishonor anyone, no matter who they are, no matter their race, no matter what lifestyle they are in, no matter what political party they belong to. Why? Because their soul is created in the image of God. Respect is due to all people, to the humblest and even to the worst. Peter says to "honor all people."

When a man or woman is considered by others to possess a respectful spirit, it is considered a noble virtue. No matter how great you become in this world, it is never acceptable to treat others disrespectfully.

Plutarch told the story of when Julius Caesar was invited into the home of a poor man in Milan for dinner:

> When at the table of Valerius Leo, who entertained him at supper at Milan, a dish of asparagus was put before him on which his host instead of oil had poured sweet ointment, Caesar partook of it without any disgust, and reprimanded his friends for finding fault with it. "For it was enough," said he, "not to eat what you did not like; but he who reflects on another man's want of breeding, shows he wants it as much himself."[25]

At that time, it was customary among people of means to use oil as a condiment for the food. But in the home of the poor, oil was not always available. Caesar, though famous throughout the world and rich and powerful, ate what the poor man put in front of him without complaint.

If you want to be respected, show respect for others and not just those whom you are trying to impress. In fact, failing to show others respect will make the one you are trying to impress to have less respect for you. Caesar told his friends that those who looked down on the poor man and his lack of refinement only showed that they lacked it just as much. The virtue of respect for others, especially toward those who may be uneducated, poor, or lack proper training, demonstrates a virtuous heart that others will admire.

---

25. Plutarch, *Lives*, 1:211.

HONESTY

> *Honest* weights and scales are the Lord's
> (Prov 16:11)

It is good to be honest when dealing with money or when taking a test. But the virtue of honesty goes far beyond ordinary truthfulness: to be honest about your feelings concerning social issues, even if it will cause others to reject you; to be honest about your faith, when your faith makes you despised; to be honest with a friend whose lifestyle is immoral and leading to their destruction, but your standing up to them might mean your rejection. Thomas Paine summed up this virtue:

> There are men too, who have not virtue enough to be angry . . . He who dares not offend cannot be honest.[26]

Honesty in business is a virtue, but the truly virtuous are honest in all areas of life. If a man or a woman is not willing to speak the truth to a friend out of fear of offending them, then he or she is playing the part of a liar. The virtue of honesty requires a person to speak the truth regardless of the results. Always strive to be virtuous in your communication—this includes being honest.

A VIRTUOUS LIFESTYLE

> But also for this very reason, giving all diligence, add to your faith *virtue* . . .
> (2 Pet 1:5)

The ancient Greek and Roman world loved and pursued virtue. It is a constant theme in ancient literature as philosophers and statesmen discussed the glories of a virtuous lifestyle.

Consider the virtuous lifestyle of Scipio. The following passage is lengthy but well worth consideration. According to Polybius, the lifestyle of Scipio consisted of three characteristics: 1. temperance 2. magnanimity 3. courage.

> The first direction taken by Scipio's ambition to lead a virtuous life, was to attain a reputation for *temperance* and excel in this respect

---

26. Paine, *Collected Writings*, 74.

all the other young men of the same age. This is a high prize indeed and difficult to gain, but it was at this time easy to pursue at Rome owing to the vicious tendencies of most of the youths. It was just at the period we are treating of that this present tendency to extravagance declared itself.... Scipio, however, setting himself to pursue the opposite course of conduct, combating all his appetites and molding his life to be in every way coherent and uniform, in about the first five years established his universal reputation for strictness and temperance. His reputation for temperance cost him nothing, but by abstaining from many and varied pleasures he gained in addition that bodily health and vigour which he enjoyed for the whole of his life, and which by the many pleasures of which it was the cause amply rewarded him for his former abstention from common pleasures....

In the next place he sedulously studied to distinguish himself from others in *magnanimity* and cleanhandedness in money matters. Scipio's goodness and generosity . . . would naturally be admired anywhere, but in Rome it was a marvel; for absolutely no one there ever gives away anything to anyone if he can help it . . .

It remained for him to gain a reputation for *courage*, nearly the most essential virtue in all states and especially so in Rome; and for this the training required of him was correspondingly severe. Chance, however, assisted him also in this determination. For the members of the royal house of Macedon had always been devoted to hunting, and the Macedonians had reserved the most suitable areas for breeding game. Aemilius, thinking that hunting was the best training and amusement for the young men, placed the royal huntsmen at Scipio's disposal, and gave him complete control over the preserves. Scipio, availing himself of this and regarding himself as being nearly in the position of king, spent the whole time that the army remained in Macedonia after the battle of Pydna in this pursuit, and, as he became a very enthusiastic sportsman, being of the right age and physique for such an exercise, like a well-bred dog, this taste of his for hunting became permanent. So that when he arrived in Rome and when he found in Polybius one equally devoted to the chase, all the time that other young men gave up to law affairs and greetings, spending the whole day in the forum and thus trying to court the favour of the populace, Scipio was occupied by the chase, and by his brilliant and memorable exploits, acquired a higher reputation than anyone. For the others could not win praise except by injuring some of their fellow-citizens, this being the usual consequence of prosecutions in the law courts; but Scipio, without ever vexing a soul, gained this universal reputation for courage, matching his deeds against their words. So that in a short space of time he had outstripped his contemporaries more than is recorded of any other Roman, although the path he pursued to gain glory was quite the opposite of that followed by all others in accordance with Roman usage and custom.[27]

The pursuit of a virtuous lifestyle will not allow one to settle for just one area of virtue, but will lead one to strive in all areas of life. Consider Plato's thought on virtue:

> Of perfect virtue there are four species: prudence, justice, bravery and temperance. Of these prudence is the cause of right conduct, justice of just dealing in partnerships and commercial transactions. Bravery is the cause which makes a man not give way but stand his ground in alarms and perils. Temperance causes mastery over desires, so that we are never enslaved by any pleasure, but lead an orderly life. Thus virtue includes first prudence, next justice, thirdly bravery, and lastly temperance.[28]

The great philosopher Epictetus had this to say on Virtue:

> Are we, then, at a loss to know how it comes about that we are subject to fear and anxiety? Why, what else can possibly happen, when we regard impending events as things evil? We cannot help but be in fear, we cannot help but be in anxiety. And then we say, "O Lord God, how may I escape anxiety?" Fool, have you not hands? Did not God make them for you? Sit down now and pray forsooth that the mucus in your nose may not run! Nay, rather wipe your nose and do not blame God! What then? Has he given you nothing that helps in the present case? Has he not given you endurance, has he not given you magnanimity, has he not given you courage? When you have such serviceable hands as these do you still look for someone to wipe your nose? But these virtues we neither practice nor concern ourselves withal.[29]

According to Epictetus, not using the virtues that God has given to us is like not using our hands to wipe our noses when they are running. Instead of just wiping our noses, we complain that God has abandoned us, even though he has endowed us with two hands to take care of the problem.

---

27. Polybius, *Histories*, Loc. 16404–86. Emphasis added.
28. Diogenes, *Lives of Eminent Philosophers*, 357.
29. Epictetus, *Discourses*, 1:317.

In the same way God has endowed mankind with the propensity to act with virtue, but most decline to use it.

PURSUING VIRTUE

To close this chapter on examples of virtue, in his autobiography Benjamin Franklin recorded his epic pursual of virtue:

> It was about this time I conceiv'd the bold and arduous project of arriving at moral perfection. I wish'd to live without committing any fault at any time; I would conquer all that either natural inclination, custom, or company might lead me into. As I knew, or thought I knew, what was right and wrong, I did not see why I might not always do the one and avoid the other. But I soon found I had undertaken a task of more difficulty than I had imagined. While my care was employ'd in guarding against one fault, I was often surprised by another; habit took the advantage of inattention; inclination was sometimes too strong for reason. I concluded, at length, that the mere speculative conviction that it was our interest to be completely virtuous, was not sufficient to prevent our slipping; and that the contrary habits must be broken, and good ones acquired and established, before we can have any dependence on a steady, uniform rectitude of conduct. For this purpose I therefore contrived the following method.
>
> In the various enumerations of the moral virtues I had met with in my reading, I found the catalogue more or less numerous, as different writers included more or fewer ideas under the same name. Temperance, for example, was by some confined to eating and drinking, while by others it was extended to mean the moderating every other pleasure, appetite, inclination, or passion, bodily or mental, even to our avarice and ambition. I propos'd to myself, for the sake of clearness, to use rather more names, with fewer ideas annex'd to each, than a few names with more ideas; and I included under thirteen names of virtues all that at that time occurr'd to me as necessary or desirable, and annexed to each a short precept, which fully express'd the extent I gave to its meaning.
>
> These names of virtues, with their precepts, were:
>
> 1. Temperance: Eat not to dullness; drink not to elevation.
> 2. Silence: Speak not but what may benefit others or yourself; avoid Trifling conversation.

3. Order: Let all your things have their places; let each part of your Business have its time.

4. Resolution: Resolve to perform what you ought; perform without fail What you resolve.

5. Frugality: Make no expense but to do good to others or yourself; i.e., Waste nothing.

6. Industry: Lose no time; be always employ'd in something useful; cut Off all unnecessary actions.

7. Sincerity: Use no hurtful deceit; think innocently and justly; and, if you Speak, speak accordingly.

8. Justice: Wrong none by doing injuries, or omitting the benefits that Are your duty.

9. Moderation: Avoid extremes; forbear resenting injuries so much as you Think they deserve.

10. Cleanliness: Tolerate no uncleanliness in body, clothes, or habitation.

11. Tranquility: Be not disturbed at trifles, or at accidents common or unavoidable.

12. Chastity: Rarely use venery but for health or offspring, never to dullness, Weakness, or the injury of your own or another's peace or Reputation.

13. Humility: Imitate Jesus and Socrates.[30]

In his pursuit of virtue, Franklin attempted to conquer each virtue on his list, one at a time. Such an endeavor is noble but impossible apart from the work of the Holy Spirit within us. As Christians, we are called to virtuous living. The virtues of the fruit of the Spirit are produced by the presence of the Holy Spirit within us. Walking in virtue empowers us to face all the circumstances of life, including trials and opposition.

---

30. Franklin, *Autobiography*, 184.

Chapter 2

Facing Trials and Opposition

My brethren, count it all joy when you fall into various *trials*, knowing that the testing of your faith produces patience.

(JAMES 1:2–3)

No one is exempt from facing trials and opposition in life, not even the virtuous. How we face trials can be its own kind of virtue. We know that trials are going to come our way in one form or another. Why do we respond with surprise and self-pity when that inevitable trial falls on us? It is not a virtuous response to be negative and complaining during the difficult times of life, and such a response certainly does not glorify God. We all have a choice for how we respond to trials. James did not say count it all joy if you *happen* to fall into a trial. He said count it joy *when* you fall into a trial. It is going to happen. Your faith is going to be tested.

Some translations have the word "trial" read "temptation." But in our day and age the word "temptation" carries with it the idea of evil or secret sin. But the Greek word here, *peirasmos*, does not mean that; it means "fiery trial." The word indicates a test that is designed to reveal the nature of the person being tested. God allows our faith to be tested; we are going to walk through fiery trials. Peter said in 1 Peter 4:12, "Beloved, do not think it strange concerning the fiery trial which is to try you, as though some strange thing happened to you."

Peter and James both tell us to expect trials. And James adds another point—not only expect them, but also be prepared for anything. He says these trials and testing of our faith will be "various." That word can be translated "multicolored." In other words, the trials of life are varied and personalized. God allows us all to be tested that we might prove our faith; the promise is that we will not be tested beyond what we are able. For one, the test may come in a doctor's diagnosis; or a child's temper tantrum; or layoffs at work; or a rebellious teenager; or a backstabbing friend. The trials are various and will come when we do not expect them.

James says to count it all joy when you "fall" into various trials. We have to live in faith, prepared for a testing at any time. We must develop the correct attitude in facing each trial. When the times of testing come, our response should not be denial or avoidance; rather we are to rejoice! James says to count it all joy. However, James is not saying that trials are joyful. Rather, James is telling us that trials become an occasion for joy when we recognize the purpose behind them.

When we are going through a fiery trial, it is not fun; it is not something that we welcome. However, the Scripture makes the case that Christians should consider faithfulness through trial as a duty. Instead of looking at trials as something with which God is punishing us, we should view the end result as an occasion for joy because of what we will learn from it.

One might paraphrase James 1:2 this way: "count your trials to be occasions of joy before they come." In other words, we are commanded to adopt that attitude now, while things are going well. We are told to realize that everyone who follows Christ will be tested, and to decide beforehand to embrace trials in light of their ultimate purpose. Always remember that dealing with adversity is one of the key ways that God tests us and prepares us to do great things for him in this world. Plutarch wrote:

> Medicine, to produce health, has to examine disease, and music, to create harmony, must investigate discord.[1]

Trials and opposition have the effect of producing Christlike character in a person's life. Someone once said, "To go high, you must go deep." Successfully navigating through the trials of life causes depth of character. Cicero once said,

---

1. Plutarch, *Lives*, 1:445.

that the loftiness of great virtues delights us, as does that of high trees, while we are not equally interested in the roots and trunks.[2]

A tall tree will not survive the thunderstorm unless it has deep roots to support its trunk. In the same way, the storms of life that will inevitably come will be used by God to give a depth of soul that will strengthen believers for even greater challenges in the future.

In Deuteronomy 8:2, Moses said to the people, "And you shall remember that the Lord your God led you all the way these forty years in the wilderness, to humble you and test you, to know what was in your heart, whether you would keep His commandments or not." The test is given to know what is in our hearts and to know whether or not we will keep God's commandments. This is one of the great purposes of trials: we can learn things about ourselves that otherwise we would never know for sure. Trials prove our faith or lack of it. Trials reveal the greatness that lies within the hearts of some, and the cowardice that lies in the hearts of others.

During World War II, Winston Churchill had great admiration for President Roosevelt. He spoke of Roosevelt's tremendous triumph over his physical disability. Roosevelt had polio and was in much pain and discomfort throughout the war. Churchill saw in Roosevelt an example of the power of trials to infuse greatness into a man's soul. He believed that God took away Roosevelt's physical strength, and instead placed within him a lion-like heart. Churchill made the connection between Roosevelt's paralysis and his courage and political passion:

> President Roosevelt's physical affliction lay heavily upon him. It was a marvel that he bore up against it through all the many years of tumult and storm. Not one man in ten millions, stricken and crippled as he was, would have attempted to plunge into a life of physical and mental exertion and of hard, ceaseless political controversy. Not one in ten millions would have tried, not one in a generation would have succeeded, not only in entering this sphere, but in becoming indisputable master of the scene. This was an extraordinary effort of the spirit over the flesh, of will-power over physical infirmity.[3]

This is one of the great purposes of trials: they expose the true heart, and it is through trials that the heart is revealed to others around us, to God, and to ourselves. Until we go through that time of trial and our

---

2. Marcellinus, *Roman History*, Loc. 1317–20.
3. Meacham, *Franklin and Winston*, 353.

commitment to the Lord that we have made with our mouths is put to the test, it has not been proven.

When Israel was in the wilderness facing starvation and death, God said to Moses in Exodus 16:4, "Behold, I will rain bread from heaven for you. And the people shall go out and gather a certain quota every day, that I may test them, whether they will walk in My law or not." The trial facing Israel was designed for self-revelation. After the trial was over, they knew who would walk according to God's Law and who would not. The trial was designed to prove them. By trusting God through this trial they knew they were God's children and confirmed that their hearts were loyal to the Lord.

When we go through trials, instead of cursing them and bitterly complaining, we need to view them as an opportunity. Most Christians say they want to honor the Lord and serve him with their lives. A trial is God's test and is an opportunity to prove our loyalty to God. It is through trials we prove our faith to ourselves. Because we trusted him when it was difficult, now we know that our heart is loyal to him. The same trials prove many to be disloyal.

THE BLESSING OF TRIALS

James wrote in the first chapter of his book, "Count it all joy when you fall into various trials." Taking joy in adversity seems like a strange thing to say, but James made it clear that there is a blessing awaiting those who face their times of trial in faith.

This is a spiritual truth, but it is also a maxim that governs the world. God has written this into the natural laws that operate in the world. All mankind will be confronted by trials, but not all respond to them as they should. We need to recognize the blessing of trials so that we will respond as we should when they come upon us. Trials and times of adversity shape our lives, depending how we respond to them. Herodotus once observed:

> No mortal existed now, nor would ever exist, who did not have a mixture of adversity in his life from the moment of his birth; indeed the greatest men encountered the greatest adversities.[4]

Herodotus spent his life researching and writing his history about great men and their achievements. He discovered that all face trials and that those who achieve the greatest successes are often those who had to

---

4. Herodotus, *Histories*, 583.

overcome the most difficult adversities. How we respond to the trials in our lives is the only thing we can control. Epictetus made this observation on overcoming adversity:

> The attainment of those things in which I can be hindered or compelled is not under my control and is neither good or bad, but the use which I make of them is either good or bad, and that is under my control.[5]

We cannot control the trials that we face in any area of our lives, and we should not consider opposition to always be bad. Trials are neutral because they are common to all of us, but how we respond to trials is either good or bad. We can choose to make good use of our trials, or we can choose to respond poorly. During the Revolutionary War, Colonel Henry Knox said:

> We want great men who, when fortune frowns, will not be discouraged.[6]

There is going to be adversity in life which must be confronted in faith. There is a purpose in trials that will be revealed in time, but it is necessary for us to wait for those results in faith and not be discouraged. It is the process of going through a trial that will produce character.

If you study the lives of some of the most famous people in history, you will soon discover that the character they are known for was the end result of the trials that they had to overcome. The trials produced the character. In his writings, Epictetus gave us the example of Heracles:

> Or what do you think Heracles would have amounted to, if there had not been a lion like the one which he encountered, and a hydra, and a stag, and a boar, and wicked and brutal men, whom he made it his business to drive out and clear away? And what would he have been doing had nothing of the sort existed? Is it not clear that he would have rolled himself up in a blanket and slept? In the first place, then, he would never have become Heracles by slumbering away his whole life in such luxury and ease; but even if he had, of what good would he have been? What would have been the use of those arms of his and of his prowess in general, and his steadfastness and nobility, had not such circumstances and occasions roused and exercised him? What then? Ought he to

---

5. Epictetus, *Discourses*, 1:233.
6. McCullough, *1776*, 201.

have prepared these for himself, and sought to bring a lion into his own country from somewhere or other, and a boar, and a hydra? This would have been folly and madness. But since they did exist and were found in the world, they were serviceable as a means of revealing and exercising our Heracles.[7]

Without such opposition, it is not too much to say that there would have been no Heracles. This is a truth that is repeated countless times throughout history. Plutarch wrote about the life of the Roman commander Sertorius, who lost his eye in battle. Losing an eye would be a severe trial for anyone. There are many who have had far lesser trials than losing an eye and never recovered. But Sertorius was different: he responded to this trial in a positive manner and considered his wound a mark of glory. Plutarch wrote of Sertorius:

> This he always esteemed an honour to him; observing that others do not continually carry about with them the marks and testimonies of their valour, but must often lay aside their chains of gold, their spears and crowns; whereas his ensigns of honour, and the manifestations of his courage, always remained with him, and those who beheld his misfortune must at the same time recognise his merits. The people also paid him the respect he deserved, and when he came into the theatre, received him with plaudits and joyful acclamations, an honour rarely bestowed even on persons of advanced standing and established reputation.[8]

Suffering trials is common to all, but our response to trials is what we can control. Trials are sometimes the catalysts that propel a person to a greater success. Napoleon had risen from obscurity to become the emperor of France. Most people know that Napoleon earned his fame because he was a highly respected general who led many successful campaigns. But what few know is that it was actually the opposition he faced that propelled him from being a general to becoming the emperor of France. Every time a plot against the life of Napoleon was discovered, it had the effect of doubling his power. General Count Philippe de Ségur was the aide-de-camp of Napoleon and witnessed many of the attempts on his life. He provided this observation:

> It is known that the principal motive alleged for the creation of the Empire was to discourage attacks on the life and temporary power

---

7. Epictetus, *Discourses*, 1:47.
8. Plutarch, *Lives*, 1:3.

Facing Trials and Opposition

of Bonaparte by making this power hereditary in his family. So that to restore the Republic or the old monarchy, there would not be one man alone to strike down but an entire dynasty.[9]

Sometimes the trials and opposition we face actually work to strengthen us and open opportunities that did not exist before. When Alexander Hamilton was a teenage boy, he was an orphan and worked as a clerk on the island of St. Croix. By that time Hamilton had already had his fair share of adversity. He was self-educated and looking for an opportunity to escape the poverty he was in.

When he was seventeen years old, the island of St. Croix was hit by an apocalyptic hurricane that destroyed virtually everything on the island. Hamilton survived the storm and decided to write a letter to the island's paper. The letter was printed, and everyone who read it was amazed that such a young man could write with such power. The letter read in part:

> It seemed as if a total dissolution of nature was taking place. The roaring of the sea and wind, fiery meteors flying about it [sic] in the air, the prodigious glare of almost perpetual lightning, the crash of the falling houses, and the ear-piercing shrieks of the distressed, were sufficient to strike astonishment into angels. . . . Where now, oh! Vile worm, is all thy boasted fortitude and resolution? What is become of thine arrogance and self sufficiency? . . . Death comes rushing on in triumph, veiled in a mantle of tenfold darkness. His unrelenting scythe, pointed and ready for the stroke . . . See thy wretched helpless state and learn to know thyself. . . . Despise thyself and adore thy God. . . . O ye who revel in affluence see the afflictions of humanity and bestow your superfluity to ease them. . . . Succour the miserable and lay up a treasure in heaven.[10]

Although Hamilton did not know it at the time, the power of his pen had written him out of his present circumstances and opened a new life for him. His letter about the hurricane created a sensation. The governor of the island located the teenage author and was motivated to send him to America to be educated.

Trials and adversity are never something that we seek out, but we would be wise to recognize the good that can come out of them. In 1845 Samuel Clemens, who would later use the name Mark Twain, was twelve years old. An epidemic of measles broke out in his hometown of Hannibal,

---

9. Ségur, *Aide-de-Camp of Napoleon*, 125.
10. Hamilton, "To The Royal Danish American Gazete."

Missouri. In this epidemic, forty citizens perished. Clemens had contracted the disease but he managed to survive. After he recovered, his mother decided to apprentice him to a printer because she thought it would be a less strenuous vocation for her son. Clemens later reflected:

> I can say with truth that the reason I am in the literary profession is because I had the measles when I was twelve years old.[11]

This is the blessing of trials. No trial is fun to go through but, as Christians, we need to recognize the providence of God over our lives. Do not curse your trials and do not shrink from times of adversity. The trials that you face may just turn out to be the means by which God opens new doors of opportunity.

TIMES THAT TRY MEN'S SOULS

When the American Revolution was in full swing and not going well for the American army, Thomas Paine wrote these words:

> These are the times that try men's souls: The summer soldier and the sunshine patriot will, in this crisis, shrink from the service of his country; but he that stands it NOW, deserves the love and thanks of man and woman. Tyranny, like hell, is not easily conquered; yet we have this consolation with us, that the harder the conflict, the more glorious the triumph. What we obtain too cheap, we esteem too lightly.[12]

As Christians, we fight a spiritual battle that is real and vicious. Opposition comes in many forms, often with hate and lies. A "summer soldier" or "sunshine patriot" refers to soldiers who only serve in between battles, when things are easy. A true solider of the Lord fights when the battle is hot. When you find yourself in a situation where it seems your soul is being tried, stand strong for the Lord and know that the struggle may be difficult, but, in the end, the Lord will not leave you or forsake you. You can do all things through Christ who strengthens you (Phil 4:13).

An even bigger temptation is to forget God during the good times or days of prosperity. In Deuteronomy 8, Moses warned the people of forgetting God and being filled with pride. Israel was about to enter into the promised land and a time of great prosperity; God had been preparing

---

11. Twain, *Autobiography*, Loc. 18392–98.
12. Paine, *Collected Writings*, 91.

Facing Trials and Opposition

them for this moment for forty years through this great test of trials. Now they were going to get their reward. But the test of trials was given as a perpetual warning against pride and self-sufficiency. Do not forget the Lord during the good times.

If you are a Christian, you need to remember all the trials and difficulties that you faced during the years of preparation. Remember all the needs you had during the days of trial, and remember all the dangers that you faced and the uncertainty about how your situation would ever change. Remember how God provided for you and met your every need.

We are all guilty of forgetting God's mercy in our lives, especially when things are going well. Most of us tend to cry out to God in desperation during times of trial. But, when we are delivered, we just praise ourselves for overcoming it, rather than thanking the Lord and acknowledging his provision.

As Charles Spurgeon said:

> We trace our joys in the sand, but we write our afflictions on marble.[13]

The wilderness was the school in which Israel had been for forty years, preparing to enter into the promised land. God knew that when they inherited that beautiful land and no longer had to rely on him to provide for them, they would forget him. In Deuteronomy 8 he warned them: do not forget. He gave them religious observances to help them: the Passover supper was a memorial of their deliverance out of Egypt, and the Feast of Tabernacles recalled their passage through the wilderness. By observing these feasts, the people would remember all the ways that God had delivered them in the past.

For us today, we need to remember the goodness of the Lord who has sustained and blessed us. Do not be tempted, as Deuteronomy 8:17 says, to say in your heart, "My power and the might of my hand have gained me this wealth."

If you have wealth today, verse 18 of that same chapter says, "And you shall remember the Lord your God, for it is He who gives you power to get wealth." In verse 10 Moses says, "When you have eaten and are full, then you shall bless the Lord."

You should be thankful to the Lord, because he is the one who has given you this wealth, and this too is a test. Will you honor the Lord during the

---

13. Spurgeon, "Pilgrim's Grateful Recollections."

blessed days? Or will you forget God? We forget God when we do not keep his commandments, when we forget God's authority over us in times of prosperity, and when we forget our obligations to him. When we grow rich, there is a danger that we start to view our faith as a needless thing. We grow content to cast it aside. Some of us grow so prideful that we think it is below us.

It is a sign of a truly ungrateful heart when the better God is to us, the more neglectful we become of him. For some of us, we have always been wealthy, we have never known hunger, we have never experienced what it is to lack material things. During the Revolutionary War, a man named Albigence Waldo wrote in his diary:

> Mankind are never truly thankfull for the Benefits of life, until they have experience'd the want of them. The Man who has seen misery knows best how to enjoy good. He who is always at ease & has enough of the Blessings of common life is an Impotent Judge of the feelings of the unfortunate.[14]

The test of trials is to prepare you for the blessings that God wants to pour into your life. But when that blessing comes, God warns you to not forget the Lord your God. Be obedient to his word and set your heart upon the word of God so that you can learn his ways and his expectations and then walk in humility and obedience and dependence on him.

Ecclesiastes 11:4 says, "He who observes the wind will not sow, and he who regards the clouds will not reap." Rather than focusing your attention on the wind and the clouds, focus on the Lord who, with a word from His mouth, can quiet the winds and remove the clouds.

We need faith in Christ to overcome obstacles in life. Do not worry about the wind and the clouds; put your faith and trust in Christ and let him guide you calmly through life. In his Memoirs, Ulysess S. Grant told the story of how he and a friend left Georgetown after purchasing a new horse:

> We got along very well for a few miles, when we encountered a ferocious dog that frightened the horses and made them run. The new animal kicked at every jump he made. I got the horses stopped, however, before any damage was done, and without running into anything. After giving them a little rest, to quiet their fears, we started again. That instant the new horse kicked, and started to run once more. The road we were on, struck the turnpike within half a mile of the point where the second runaway commenced, and there was an embankment twenty or more feet

---

14. Waldo, "Diary," 402.

deep on the opposite side of the pike. I got the horses stopped on the very brink of the precipice. My new horse was terribly frightened and trembled, Every time I attempted to start, my new horse would commence to kick. I was in quite a dilemma for a time. Once in Maysville I could borrow a horse from an uncle who lived there; but I was more than a day's travel from that point. Finally I took out my bandanna—the style of handkerchief in universal use then—and with this blindfolded my horse. In this way I reached Maysville safely the next day.[15]

Some of us are like that horse: we kick and jump and are afraid at every turn, we shudder and tremble at every dark cloud, and every time the wind blows we cower in fear. What we need is to put on a blindfold and put our faith and trust in Jesus Christ.

You can always discern a believer who is living in genuine faith; they are fearless and attempt great things for God. They are not petty and negative and small-minded because genuine faith causes us to overcome life's obstacles.

REMOVE INIMICAL PROCEEDINGS

> Two are better than one, because they have a good reward for their labor. For if they fall, one will lift up his companion. But woe to him who is alone when he falls, for he has no one to help him up ... though one may be overpowered by another, two can withstand him. And a threefold cord is not quickly broken.
> (Eccl 4:9–10, 12)

Another type of trial that we face is opposition from other people. In the fourth chapter of Ecclesiastes, Solomon laid out the benefits of having friends and being connected to others. In all areas of life, it is always better for you personally if you make friends and avoid making enemies. Sometimes, if treated correctly, an enemy may become a friend.

Whether in work or in sports, you will have to deal with the inevitable slights and hurts that will come from peers. How you respond to such opposition will affect how others view you, so it is vital that you respond in a way that honors God and also puts you in a position to come out victorious.

When Benjamin Franklin was a young man, trying to make his way professionally, he found himself being opposed by someone who, from a

---

15. Grant, *Memoirs*, 9.

Seeking Virtue

worldly perspective, had an upper hand on him. In 1736, Franklin was chosen to be clerk of the General Assembly. That year, the choice was made without opposition. The following year he was up for the same position, but a new member of the Assembly rose and made a speech against Franklin and in support of another candidate.

The man who opposed Franklin was a gentleman of fortune and education with many great talents. He was soon to be a leading politician, and he was just the kind of man of whom many would have been envious and jealous. Franklin was a student of human behavior, and he studied how to win and influence friends. He was not an envious type. Franklin devised a method to win that man as a friend. He related this experience in his autobiography:

> Having heard that he had in his library a certain very scarce and curious book, I wrote a note to him expressing my desire of perusing that book and requesting he would do me the favour of lending it to me for a few days. He sent it immediately and I return'd it in about a week with another note expressing strongly my sense of the favour. When we next met in the House he spoke to me (which he had never done before), and with great civility; and he ever after manifested a readiness to serve me on all occasions, so that we became great friends and our friendship continued to his death. This is another instance of the truth of an old maxim I had learned, which says, "He that has once done you a kindness will be more ready to do you another than he whom you yourself have obliged." And it shows how much more profitable it is prudently to remove, than to resent, return, and continue inimical proceedings.[16]

Franklin met this opposition with wisdom and patience. He did not respond with a defensive spirit, which would have made him look small and bitter. Instead of putting on a show of false humility, or cowering down, feeling less equal to the man opposing him, Franklin addressed him as an equal and treated him with respect. The result was blessing. Franklin made a lifelong friend who helped him for the rest of his life. This all came from borrowing a book and sharing a common interest.

---

16. Franklin, *Autobiography*, 212.

Facing Trials and Opposition

DEALING WITH WOLVES

Dealing with difficult people is a trial that is common to all those who seek to live for the Lord. You will discover anytime you attempt to achieve anything in life that, inevitably, there will be opposition.

There are some people who experience a perverted sense of joy in attacking those who are attempting to do great things for God. They will always come to you as though they are just one representing many. They will say something like, "Well, I am just telling you what I heard . . ." or, "A lot of people are against you on this . . ." Consider the experience of Ulysses S. Grant before you let fear of opposition cause you to let go of your dreams:

> On the evening of the first day out from Goliad we heard the most unearthly howling of wolves, directly in our front. The prairie grass was tall and we could not see the beasts, but the sound indicated that they were near. To my ear it appeared that there must have been enough of them to devour our party, horses and all, at a single meal. The part of Ohio that I hailed from was not thickly settled, but wolves had been driven out long before I left. Benjamin was from Indiana, still less populated, where the wolf yet roamed over the prairies. He understood the nature of the animal and the capacity of a few to make believe there was an unlimited number of them. He kept on towards the noise, unmoved. I followed in his trail, lacking moral courage to turn back and join our sick companion. I have no doubt that if Benjamin had proposed returning to Goliad, I would not only have "seconded the motion" but have suggested that it was very hard-hearted in us to leave Augur sick there in the first place; but Benjamin did not propose turning back. When he did speak it was to ask; "Grant, how many wolves do you think there are in that pack?" Knowing where he was from, and suspecting that he thought I would overestimate the number, I determined to show my acquaintance with the animal by putting the estimate below what possibly could be correct, and answered: "Oh, about twenty," very indifferently. He smiled and rode on. In a minute we were close upon them, and before they saw us. There were just two of them. Seated upon their haunches, with their mouths close together, they had made all the noise we had been hearing for the past ten minutes. I have often thought of this incident since when I have heard the noise of a few disappointed politicians who had deserted their associates. There are always more of them before they are counted.[17]

---

17. Grant, *Memoirs*, 35–36.

There will always be opposition as you attempt to achieve great things in life. But, if you are doing what is right and virtuous, do not be fearful of the chatter of naysayers. They are always less numerous than the awful noise they make. The stinging words of those who oppose us will actually strengthen our resolve, if we will respond in faith. Anytime we are forced to struggle through opposition, it will have the effect of making us stronger and even more prepared for greater adversity that will come in the future. The great philosopher Epictetus made this insightful observation:

> Is it possible, then, to derive advantage from these things? Yes, from everything. Even from the man who reviles me? And what good does his wrestling-companion do the athlete? The very greatest. So also my reviler becomes one who prepares me for my contest; he exercises my patience, my dispassionateness, my gentleness.[18]

According to Epictetus, the opposition of other people exercises and strengthens our virtues in the same way that a wrestler is made stronger by battling his opponent in the ring.

FIGHTING SPIRITUAL BATTLES

> Put on the whole armor of God, that you may be able to stand against the wiles of the devil.
> (Eph 6:11)

The most difficult form of opposition you will ever face is spiritual opposition from the enemy of our souls. We are fighting a spiritual battle, and we are expected by our Commander to not only fight and survive, but also to win. Winston Churchill made the following observation from his experience in World War II:

> How easy to destroy. How hard to build. How easy to evacuate, how hard to capture. How easy to do nothing. How hard to achieve anything. War is action, energy & hazard. These sheep only want to browse among the daisies.[19]

Do not be caught browsing among the daisies, because we are here on a mission from our heavenly Commander. Yes, there will be opposition, but through hard work and faith we cannot fail. You only live once; this is your

---

18. Epictetus, *Discourses*, 2:119.
19. Gilbert, *Churchill*, 349–50.

Facing Trials and Opposition

chance to serve the Lord with all of your heart. Follow the rule of conduct of Admiral Lord Fisher:

> Moderation in war is folly. If you strike, strike hard and wherever you can.[20]

In the same way, Christians need to guard against always being on the defensive. In the current age, Christians are made to feel guilty for believing in the doctrines of God's word, especially those that touch on sensitive social issues. As a result, many true believers hide their faith publicly. They do not want to be called on to answer difficult questions that will put them in danger of being attacked by a politically correct world. When they are confronted, they are on the defensive, trying to soften what the world views as the rigid doctrines of the New Testament and the judgmental God of the Old Testament.

Have we forgotten that we are in a spiritual war? Have we forgotten what we are fighting for? The souls of family, neighbors, friends, and co-workers are at stake. The church needs to awaken to the truth that we were not given the spiritual body-armor described in Ephesians 6 for the purpose of hiding from our enemies. We have been armed with the sword of the Spirit, which is the word of God.

You can use your sword for defense, but a coward will not put up much of a fight, even if he is armed with a powerful and sharp sword. Christians must stand and fight. When confronted about our faith, we must be ready to use the weapons that God has provided.

In Act IV of Shakespeare's *Julius Caesar*, Brutus and Cassius debate whether to attack their enemies immediately or to wait for another time. Brutus, arguing for a quick strike, utters these famous lines: "There is a tide in the affairs of men; which, taken at the flood, leads to fortune; Omitted, all the voyage of their life; Is bound in shallows and in miseries."[21]

In other words, when the opportunity is there, take it, or else you will be destined to obscurity and spiritual boredom. Christians need to recognize the tide in their life; if God has placed you in a position to catch the tide and do something for him, do not passively wait.

Are you ready? Has God placed you in a battlefield at a strategic moment? No matter where you are, act as you should, live with purpose, and

---

20. Churchill, "Grand Alliance," 54.
21. Shakespeare, *Julius Caesar*, 3.3.18–21.

find that tide that is rolling and jump on. The worst thing you can do is be passive.

Esther fought one of the toughest spiritual battles recorded in the Bible. She was taking on the most powerful men in the most dominant empire in the ancient world. Her uncle, Mordecai, discovered the plot of the wicked Haman to destroy himself and the Jews. Esther, who had been chosen as the queen of Persia, was in the palace when her uncle called on her and delivered the news. In Esther 4:14, the words of her uncle spoke to her heart: "Yet who knows whether you have come to the kingdom for such a time as this."

Once Esther had recognized the moment and fasted and prayed to the Lord, she decided in her heart that the battlefield on which she found herself was from the Lord. Esther resolved to directly approach the king, even if it meant her own life. That is courage. Courage is the ability to conquer fear. Esther said, "If I perish, I perish" (Esth 4:16).

Some say there are two types of courage. One is called animal courage. Animal courage is the result of nerves that have been driven to the breaking point. This type of courage is brought on by desperation, not out of personal choice and conviction.

The other kind is moral courage. Moral courage is seen in one who, after considering the options, makes a convictional decision to face the danger, even if it costs them everything.

If a young man is drafted into the army without choice, he is on the battlefield and must drum up the courage. That is animal courage. But it is moral courage when a young man or woman, out of patriotism and a sense of duty, knowing the danger, still volunteers for the battle. It is the courage of the highest order when one faces death after cool reflection. That was the courage of the martyrs in the early church.

It was also the courage of Esther. Esther was resolved to go to the king. Her resolve was not the result of absolute desperation. She did not crumble under the weight of the difficulty because her resolution was the result of a recognition of God's providence. After counting the cost and seeking the help of God, she braved the danger.

We are reminded of the many men and women martyrs who were called on to face the most fearful consequences for their faith and did so, knowing beforehand of the danger.

Martin Luther, the great Reformer, was dragged before a religious council with the Holy Roman Emperor Charles V presiding. Luther was commanded to recant his written works and his views on the doctrine of justification. He asked for time to think about it. They gave him twenty-four hours. After a night of prayer and time with God, Luther appeared the next day, believing that he would die unless he recanted. It was at this time that he uttered these famous words: "Here I stand; I can do no other. God help me, Amen."

The spirit displayed by Luther was also in Esther. Make no mistake: this is the spirit that is demanded by Jesus Christ our Savior in each one of us. Without that same kind of commitment, we cannot be his disciples. Jesus said in Luke 14:26–27, "If anyone comes to Me and does not hate his father and mother, wife and children, brothers and sisters, yes, and his own life also, he cannot be My disciple. And whoever does not bear his cross and come after Me cannot be My disciple." Christian, you may not be called upon to actually make the ultimate sacrifice, but you cannot live your life on the spiritual battlefield without the readiness to lay it down.

Another form of spiritual trial that we face arises from our own neglect of following the Lord. When we make bad choices in life or we neglect following the Word of God, trials will come. The Lord will send times of testing upon us to see if we will be faithful to him or not.

The Jewish rabbis used to teach that adversity was allowed into the lives of God's people if they neglected studying the Scripture. Rabbi Hisda, whose teachings are recorded in the Talmud, made this observation:

> Upon whoever has the possibility of taking up the study of Torah and does not do so, the Holy One, blessed be he, brings ugly and troubling suffering. . . . If a person sees that sufferings afflict him, let him examine his deeds. "For it is said, 'Let us search and try our ways and return to the Lord' (Lam. 3:40). "If he examined his ways and found no cause [for his suffering], let him blame the matter on his wasting [time better spent in studying] the Torah. "For it is said, 'Happy is the man whom you chastise, O Lord, and teach out of your Torah' (Ps. 94:12).[22]

There are many forms of spiritual trials that come upon a child of God. We need to make sure that our trial is not one of our own making.

---

22. Neusner, *Babylonian Talmud*, 21.

THE TRIAL OF SICKNESS

Another kind of trial that we face is physical illness. I believe God uses sickness and illness to prepare us for death. Some will experience sudden death without warning. But, for most others, they will slip into the next world after a long bout with sickness and illness, and God has ordained it to be this way.

There is a purpose in the suffering and illnesses that lead to our deaths. What is that purpose? To prepare us for what happens after we die. God in his grace uses sickness and pain to prepare us for the life and the judgment to come. Think of the ways that God uses sickness and illness to prepare us for heaven.

Sickness elevates our hearts out of the world

When our health goes, so does our love for the world. It is natural for us to want to preserve life and our health. But, as a result, we tend to hold on to the love of this world so tightly that we get to the point where we are unwilling to leave it. Sickness is God's cure for the love of the world. For the believer, as the sickness that leads to death runs its course, we are able to say, "Praise God that it is over, praise God that their soul has been released."

My grandmother died when she was ninety years old. For ninety years, she lived a faithful Christian life, but for five years she dealt with illness. Sickness gripped her body to the point that she was bedridden. She longed for heaven, and her family was ready for God to take her. There is an element of grace in sickness. It takes away our love for the world and elevates our heart to heaven.

Sickness causes us to turn from sin

The Bible teaches us that we are made perfect through our sufferings. Sometimes, those sufferings are in the form of illness due to sin, and the sickness is God correcting his child. In 1 Corinthians 11:30, the apostle Paul spoke of those who became ill because they were partaking of the Lord's Supper in a way that was displeasing to the Lord. I believe that God uses illness and disease to cause us to turn to him and forsake sin.

It is a tragedy when unbelievers get a sickness that will lead to death and still persist in closing their heart to God. That sickness was allowed by the Lord to awaken the person to a chance to change and to accept Christ. Of course, not every illness is the result of sin. Just ask Job. All suffering has the effect of causing us to turn from sin and rely on God. Someone has said, "While all affliction is a school, the last illness should be the finishing school." In other words, we need to learn during times of adversity. When a sickness or incurable disease comes upon us, it motivates us to turn from our sin and to seek the Lord.

Sickness prepares us for death and judgment

Sickness is God's way of reminding all of us that we will one day die. Our bodies in their present state will not live forever. Every illness is the herald of God, the trumpet of warning. It is our body calling out to us, "Prepare your soul, sinner; get your house in order and prepare to meet your God." Unfortunately, most people refuse to hear.

There is an old German fable that warns us to open our eyes and ears to the warnings of God. Death promised a young man that he would not summon him until he had first sent several messengers to warn him of his coming. So the young man took his fill of pleasure and sin and wasted his health in hard partying and gluttony. It did not take long for an illness to come upon him. He was laid up sick for a while, but since no messenger had appeared, he had no worries. When he recovered, he went right back to his sinful life.

Over the years he had a number of sicknesses and maladies that would come upon him, but, remembering his covenant with death, he made light of them. He said each time, "I am not going to die anytime soon, the first messenger has yet to come." But, one day, unexpectedly, someone tapped him on the shoulder. He turned, and there stood the hooded figure of death at his shoulder. Death, the king of terror said, "Follow me, the hour of thy departure is come." The young man said, "How is this? You have not kept your word! You promised to send me messengers, and I have never seen one."

Death bellowed out in his hideous voice, "Silence! . . . I have sent you messenger after messenger. What was the fever? What was that sickness and that disease? What was each of those illnesses that came upon you? Each one was a herald; each was my messenger."[23]

---

23. Spence and Exell, *I and II Kings*, 12.

God uses sickness to warn of us death, to take the world out of our hearts, to prepare us for and remind us of coming judgment. Have you heeded that warning? Have you set your house in order? Have you done business with God while there is still daylight left? Decide today to no longer turn a deaf ear and heed the warning.

GOOD JUDGMENT

> If God is for us, who can be against us?
> (Rom 8:31)

Some of us are crippled with fear and the cause of it is our own poor judgment. Our poor judgment causes us to fear things that we have no business fearing, and it causes us to not fear things that should cause our hearts to melt.

The ancient Greek philosopher Epictetus argued that it is our ability to practice good judgment that will make the difference in overcoming fears. He argued that our fear is oftentimes misplaced and as a result we make things out to be far worse than they actually are:

> For example, whenever I go to sea, on gazing down into the deep or looking around upon the expanse of waters and seeing no land, I am beside myself, fancying that if I am wrecked I shall have to swallow this whole expanse of waters; but it does not occur to me that three pints are enough. What is it, then, that disturbs me? The expanse of sea? No, but my judgement. Again, when there is an earthquake, I fancy that the whole city is going to fall upon me; what, is not a little stone enough to knock my brains out? What, then, are the things that weigh upon us and drive us out of our senses? Why, what else but our judgements?[24]

Our poor judgment causes us to fear things that we have no business fearing. If God is my strength, what in this world can possibly cause me to fear? But our poor judgment causes us to forget to fear what we should really be fearing. We should fear opposing and offending our heavenly Father. We should be fearful of sin destroying us, not a storm flooding us. What can a storm do to my soul? God is the one who truly has all the power; he is the one who by his word can calm the storm. We should not be fearing the storm, but the one who can control it. If God possesses all strength, let

---

24. Epictetus, *Discourses*, 1:319.

us be like the psalmist (Ps 27:1), "Lord you are the strength of my life; Of whom shall I be afraid?"

When we reflect on the trials and adversity that we face in life, we need to utilize good judgment. Jesus said in John 16:33, "In this world you will have trouble, but take heart, I have overcome the world." If we are using good judgment, we will recognize that trials are to be expected and received in faith.

Never forget that some of God's richest blessings come on the other side of trials. Jesus said in Matthew 5:4, "Blessed are those who mourn, for they will be comforted." Jesus does not mean, "Blessed are miserable, negative Christians." Some believers, of course, choose to live that way. It is wrong for a believer to live life with a negative, bitter spirit. It is bad for the church; it is bad for your family; and it is death for your witness to the world. People in the world mock Christians who are negative. Robert Louis Stevenson once wrote, ironically, in his diary, "I've been to church today and am not depressed."[25] Apparently, that was the exception to the rule.

The mourners that Jesus refers to here are in spiritual mourning. There are bad types of mourning and there is a mourning that reveals genuine Christian conviction. A mourning for our own sins is godly sorrow. Zechariah 12:10 says, "And I will pour on the house of David and on the inhabitants of Jerusalem the Spirit of grace and supplication; then they will look on Me whom they pierced. Yes, they will mourn for Him as one mourns for his only son, and grieve for Him as one grieves for a firstborn." God's mourners are those who live a life of repentance; in this sense, mourning is a part of the Christian life. Our bodies groan because of sin.

It reveals the state of a person's heart when they do not mourn over sin. When a believer chooses to sin, it leads to a heaviness of conviction. We know our holy God, and we know what he has done for us and how much he loves us. When we fail, our spirit groans in conviction and regret.

The mourning of which Jesus speaks is a personal thing; it is in the heart of a true believer who desires to please their heavenly Father. It also refers to the mourning that is the result of the sin around us, which we observe in the world. It is the mourning of those who "weep with those who weep," or the sorrow over the souls of those who are perishing in their sins. As Christ mourned over Jerusalem, we mourn over our cities, our country, our friends, and our families who have rejected the truth.

---

25. Stevenson, *Selected Letters*, 219.

David mourned for the sins of others in Psalm 119:136: "Rivers of water run down from my eyes, because men do not keep Your law." The great Jeremiah, the weeping prophet, wept for his people.

Now we begin to see the meaning of the paradox of the second Beatitude: "Blessed are those who mourn, for they will be comforted." Now understand, this does not mean that Christians are to be long-faced and depressed. This mourning speaks of conviction; if it is genuine, it should be in the heart. If the only time we mourn over sin is when others are watching, what does that say about the genuineness of our faith?

God wants us to be happy and positive people. Humor and laughter are good and necessary for the believer. Solomon says that a merry heart acts as "good medicine" (Prov 17:22). Laughter is essential, but so is conviction. There is a time to laugh; so is there a time to cry. It is wrong for us to approach life as one big party when so much of life for most people is filled with suffering.

Some Christians decide in their affluence and wealth to refuse to take in unpleasant news. They live without conviction. They laugh when there is no reason to laugh. In fact, they laugh when they ought to cry. What we laugh about and what we cry about reveals the spiritual condition of our hearts. The world runs mindlessly after pleasure and amusement, but the Lord says, "Blessed are they that mourn." Then he gives the promise, "they shall be comforted."

There are going to be trials that come upon us. As followers of Christ let us accept in faith the fiery trial that comes upon us. God is on our side. We are his children, and God will give us the strength we need to overcome.

AN OCCASION FOR PRAYER

The ultimate blessing that trials bring into the life of a believer is that they drive us to our knees in prayer. There is nothing more motivating than adversity to make us a people of prayer. God expects us to pray to him when we go through a trial, and he has given us precious promises in his word that he will bless us when we turn to him in our hour of need.

In 1 Kings 8, we read about the beautiful ceremony that took place on the day that Solomon dedicated the temple in Jerusalem. The chapter divides easily into three parts. The first part was the ceremony of bringing in the ark of the covenant and installing it into the Holy of Holies in the temple. God's presence was manifested by the bright cloud that filled the

Facing Trials and Opposition

sanctuary as soon as the ark was placed there. The second part was the great speech of Solomon, which mostly was a long and beautiful prayer. Solomon uttered this prayer while on his knees with his hands outstretched toward God, whose physical presence was in the temple. The third part was when Solomon rose to his feet, turned to all the people, and pronounced a blessing on the congregation.

Solomon spoke to them and explained the purpose of the temple in verses 15–21; when you read that passage, you will see the word "name" mentioned five times. The temple is the place of God's name. God dwells in the place that is reserved for his name, God is concerned about his name, and it is the purpose of God's covenant people to make his name famous throughout all the world.

This passage reveals something awesome and terrible for us today. It is awesome because we learn where God's presence is, but terrible because of how some of us are acting in his presence. Where is the Spirit of God today? He is in his temple, but where is his temple?

Our bodies are the temple of the Holy Spirit of God. First Corinthians 3:16–17 makes that very point: "Do you not know that you are the temple of God and that the Spirit of God dwells in you? If anyone defiles the temple, God will destroy him. For the temple of God is holy, which temple you are."

Could you imagine someone lusting in their heart on that day when God's cloud descended on the temple? Could you imagine any of those people counting their money or gorging themselves with food or drink? No, they were in awe; they were in prayer. Our bodies are the temples of the Holy Spirit of God; when we come together God is present. He is powerful and holy, and we must dedicate our bodies to the Lord. Let nothing defile the temple of God. Dedicate yourself through baptism and holiness, and let nothing come into your body through your eyes that would defile the temple.

In Solomon's day, the temple was a physical building, and it was there that God dwelt. Solomon prayed to God and listed out seven different trials the people would face that would become occasions for prayer: sin against neighbor, defeat by enemies, drought, famine, pestilence, besieged by enemies, and sickness. Solomon prayed in 1 Kings 8:38–39, "Whatever prayer, whatever supplication is made by anyone, or by all your people Israel, when each one knows the plague of his own heart, and spreads out his hands toward this Temple: then hear from heaven Your dwelling place, and forgive, and act, and give to everyone according to all his ways, whose heart You know (for You alone know the hearts of all the sons of men)."

This is what you must do: stretch out your arms to Jesus today. You cannot cure that plague on your own. You have been trying for years and it has not worked. You said to yourself, "I will never sin like that again." But, like a dog returns to its vomit, you renege on your vows and go right back into that sin that is plaguing your heart. You cannot stop it, and it will not go away on its own. More money will not fix it. Changing churches will not cure it. You must turn to the Great Physician for healing. God is the one who made you, and he is the only one who can fix you. After you turn to him, like Solomon, get down on your knees and stretch out your arms to him.

Solomon's prayer had a dual function: it was a prayer to God, but it was instructional to God's people. Solomon prayed that the content of his prayer would be before the Lord day and night. He asked that God would remember it constantly so that when one of his people turned to the temple with outstretched arms, God would remember this prayer and act on it.

Solomon prayed that God would "maintain the cause of His people Israel, as each day may require." What this means is that this is a present reality for all of us: God is on his throne; Jesus is our temple; and when we pray to him, Jesus stands ready to maintain our cause. He is available for help through anything we go through, as each day may require. Every day there is something new that we must face, different challenges for different days. God has promised to maintain our cause, and there is grace for every circumstance of every day.

Paul called it the manifold grace of God. Whatever you need for the troubles of this day, God will supply, but you must go to him. You must carve out the time to be with your Lord and Savior. Each day brings with it its own set of circumstances, but God never gives wrong instructions.

If you are struggling against some form of sin or lust, God will maintain your cause. He extends his hand to steady you and keep you from falling. But, you must die to yourself before you can be free to live for Jesus. Go outside and lift up your face to the heavens; stretch out your arms and praise him for saving you. Declare that the old man is dead. Now, you can live for him, and God will maintain your cause.

Are you anxiety-filled today? Look to Jesus and he will maintain your cause; he will remind you to be anxious for nothing. Believe the words of Paul in Philippians 4:6–7, "Be anxious for nothing, but in everything by prayer and supplication, with thanksgiving, let your requests be made known to God; and the peace of God which surpasses all understanding, will guard your hearts and minds through Christ Jesus." Whatever you need on any given day, God stands ready to maintain your cause. Only make sure your cause and the Lord's cause are one and the same.

One of the most beautiful examples given in the Scripture of a man crying out to God during a trial is King Hezekiah, the king of Judah, when the armies of Sennachrib were threatening to destroy Jerusalem. Sennachrib sent a letter to Hezekiah, warning him to surrender and put no trust in his God to deliver him.

The story is found in 2 Kings 19. Hezekiah was in serious trouble and knew that his only hope was divine intervention. Hezekiah did exactly what Solomon prayed during the dedication of the temple. He spread the threatening letter out before the Lord inside the temple. Hezekiah also laid out the argument as to why God should answer his prayer and deliver him from this pagan king. Hezekiah argued that the Assyrians did not believe that the God of Israel was real or that he would answer their prayer. Hezekiah prayed and said, "You are God, you alone, of all the kingdoms of the earth. You have made heaven and earth."

Hezekiah made two solid arguments in this prayer: first, he argued that God should deliver Israel for his own name's sake. Secondly, he argued that, if God did not act, these unbelievers would be confirmed in their own minds that God is not real. It was for God's glory that Hezekiah argued.

Note the contrast between the two kings. The Assyrian king was boastful and arrogant; he insulted God and called him a liar. He stood in all his pride and arrogance and believed his massive army was all he needed. But Hezekiah, alone in the house of God, spread out a letter, got on his knees, and humbled himself before God. Who do you think God is going to answer? Do you think God is going to let his humble servant go through this alone? Not in a million years.

And so it is for us; let the world boast and accuse us; but let us go into the house of the Lord and lay it all out before him. Let us make our case to the Lord, "God, I do what I do for you and your glory." "God, if you do not help me it will reflect poorly on your name. God, help me, I trust in you."

Hezekiah, then, did a wise thing in going to the place where blessing was to be found. He spread the letter before the Lord. What a lesson this is for us all! The best thing we can do with our difficulties is to spread them out before God.

God heard the prayer of Hezekiah and he acted. The entire army of Sennachrib was destroyed by the Lord. It is interesting to note that the destruction of this army is confirmed by sources outside of the Bible. Josephus said it was done by a pestilential disease, which was instant death to them. This army's destruction was also referenced by the ancient historian, Herodotus:

> An army of field mice swarmed through their camp and chewed up their quivers, bowstrings and even the handles of their shields, so that on the next day, the enemy found themselves deprived of their weapons and defenseless; many fell as they tried to flee."[26]

Mice are a Greek symbol of pestilence. However it happened, it was the hand of God that destroyed this Assyrian army. God was true to his word, and he honored the humility of Hezekiah. Hezekiah faced an impossible situation, and he responded by seeking refuge in the house of the Lord. He went to the house of the Lord to seek wise counsel, to pray, and to hear and receive a word from the Lord. Because of his faith and trust, the Lord answered his prayers. It is no different for us. Let us leave the world and hide ourselves in the house of the Lord.

---

26. Herodotus, *Histories*, 182.

Chapter 3

Achieving Greatness

Whoever desires to become *great* among you, let him be your servant.
(MATTHEW 20:26)

There is a certain virtue in those who achieve greatness in this world. To be great at something usually means that the person has made personal sacrifices that inspire admiration. Jesus introduced a new way of looking at greatness in this world. According to Jesus, the truly great man or woman is one who is the most humble and the most willing to serve. If you will study the lives of great men and women through the ages, you will notice some shared characteristics in their lives that contributed to their achieving greatness in this world.

By any worldly standard one of the greatest men who ever lived was George Washington. But, as great as he was, he could not guarantee his own successes. Success is a mysterious mix of luck, hard work, and divine providence. Washington enjoyed theatrical productions, and his favorite was entitled *Cato*. One line in particular he quoted frequently as president:

> Tis not in mortals to command success, but we'll do more, Sempronius, we'll deserve it.[1]

---

1. McCullough, *1776*, 47.

You can be great without being successful in the eyes of the world. You cannot control the results of your endeavors, but you can control your actions. You might not be able to guarantee success, but you can deserve it. The quotes and stories in this chapter will illuminate ways in which you can deserve success and, ultimately, achieve greatness in the eyes of your Creator.

FOCUS

> Let your eyes look straight ahead, and your eyelids look right before you. Ponder the path of your feet, and let all your ways be established. Do not turn to the right or the left; remove your foot from evil.
> (Prov 4:25–27)

You will never achieve greatness if you are distracted by superficial things that are not related to your field of endeavor. Time is precious, and if you are wasting your time on frivolous pursuits, you will not be able to focus on what is most important. Benjamin Franklin once stated:

> I have always thought that one man of tolerable abilities may work great changes, and accomplish great affairs among mankind if he first forms a good plan and, cutting off all amusements or other employments that would divert his attention, makes the execution of that same plan his sole study and business.[2]

One of the keys to success is focus. Whether in business, ministry, or in any endeavor you undertake, there will always be competition and opposition. Even if you are not the most naturally talented, if you will focus on the task at hand and put away those things that do not contribute to reaching your goals, you can achieve greatness. But, you must focus and remove those things that distract.

Not only do you need to focus on what is most important, you must also focus on making sure that your actions line up with your words. Valerius Maximus stated on that subject:

> Socrates also used to say that there was a quick and short road for those who wanted to attain glory: they would have to make sure that they would in fact be the type of people they wanted others to

---

2. Franklin, *Autobiography*, 203.

imagine they were. With this statement he clearly warned people to seize virtue itself rather than chase after its shadow.[3]

If you want to achieve a measure of greatness, and if you want to find favor in the eyes of God and your peers, you must be focused. Dream great dreams, set lofty goals, and focus your choices and actions on meeting those goals. Turn away from things that would keep you from achieving your goals. And above all, focus on actually being the person that you want other people to think you are. Do not play the hypocrite. Do not make people think you are a certain kind of person when if they could look into your heart they would discover you are only playacting.

PAY THE PRICE

> Let no one despise your youth, but be an example to the believers in word, in conduct, in love, in spirit, in faith, in purity. Till I come, give attention to reading, to exhortation, to doctrine. Do not neglect the gift that is in you . . . meditate on these things, give yourself entirely to them, that your progress may be evident to all.
> (1 Tim 4:12–15)

If a person desires to achieve greatness in any area of life, there will be a price to pay. If you want to be a major-league hitter, you have to pay the price in the batting cage with countless hours of work. If you want to be great in any business, you will have to pay the price behind the desk. If you want to be the greatest servant of God, there is a price to pay. Jesus said that you will have to be a servant of all.

Alexander Hamilton became one of the greatest leaders in early America. His road to greatness required that he pay the price in educating himself, due to the fact that he did not have the opportunity for formal education. As a young man, through the providential hand of God in his life, he found himself on the staff of General George Washington. In this position, Hamilton had very little time to himself to pursue personal desires. Through amazing discipline and focus, Hamilton prepared himself for the future.

There was no reason for anyone to assume that the young Alexander Hamilton would develop into the man that he became. When one reads about his early years, it reads like a list of what no child should experience.

3. Maximus, *Memorable Deeds and Sayings*, 239.

Seeking Virtue

In his formative years, his father left home never to be seen again, his mother died, his cousin who took him in committed suicide; his aunt, uncle, and grandmother had all died. By the age of fourteen he was alone, with no friends and no money. In the following years, his experience was filled with negative people who did little to help him.

It is hard to imagine that childhood experiences such as this could produce such a brilliant man. But, as is often the case with those who experience hardship at a young age, their personalities are marked by a deeper and more thoughtful character.

Hamilton shared another characteristic that is common with great men and women: as a young child he was very serious-minded. While other boys his age were playing and getting into various kinds of trouble, he chose to work hard. Hamilton read anything he could find, especially works of history and political philosophy.

God is able to take our trials and our difficult circumstances and use them to fashion us into a vessel to be used by him. People who do great things in this world often possess a serious mind as a youth, and this was the case with Hamilton. Even as a young man serving with Washington during the Revolutionary War, Hamilton used every spare moment to educate himself. As he served on General Washington's staff, he was very busy, but used his extra time to read. He kept detailed notes of the books he read, and these notes would fill up volumes. Hamilton's biographer described the content of his extensive reading:

> Like the other founding fathers, Hamilton rummaged through the wisdom of antiquity for political precedents. From the First Philippic of Demosthenes, he plucked a passage that summed up his conception of a leader as someone who would not pander to popular whims. "As a general marches at the head of his troops," so should wise politicians "march at the head of affairs, insomuch that they ought not to wait the event to know what measures to take, but the measures which they have taken ought to produce the event." Nearly fifty-one pages of the pay book contain extracts from a six-volume set of Plutarch's Lives. Thereafter, Hamilton always interpreted politics as an epic tale from Plutarch of lust and greed and people plotting for power. Since his political theory was rooted in his study of human nature, he took special delight in Plutarch's biographical sketches. And he carefully noted the creation of senates, priesthoods, and other elite bodies that governed the lives of the people.[4]

---

4. Chernow, *Alexander Hamilton*, 110.

ACHIEVING GREATNESS

Alexander Hamilton paid the price to achieve his dreams. For Hamilton that price consisted of little sleep and few parties with friends. Had Hamilton indulged himself in socializing, he would not have achieved this great feat in self-education.

It is always best if you pay the price when you are young. It becomes much more difficult when you are older to find the time to pursue knowledge on the path to greatness. If you study the lives of the greatest men and women in history, this is a common thread in their lives: even in their youth they were different than other kids in that they pursued greatness rather than wasting time playing the games of children.

For all Christians, though we have fun and enjoy life, there should be an underlying seriousness in how we live. We know this world will not last forever. The day of judgment will soon come; therefore we live life in a serious and purposeful manner. This is a characteristic of great people, who even as youths do not fall into the common vices of other young people their age.

Plutarch recorded this concerning the great Greek leader Themistocles:

> It is confessed by all that from his youth he was a vehement and impetuous nature, of a quick apprehension, and a strong and aspiring bent for action and great affairs. The holidays and intervals in his studies he did not spend in play or idleness, as other children, but would be always inventing or arranging some oration or declamation to himself, the subject of which was generally the excusing or accusing his companions, so that his master would often say to him, "You, my boy, will be nothing small, but great one way or other, for good or else for bad."[5]

Consider the life of Alexander the Great from the works of Arrian:

> He had an extraordinary physical beauty and hardihood and an exceedingly shrewd and courageous spirit; he was unsurpassed in his love of honor, his zest for danger, and his scrupulous attention to the rites of the gods. With regard to bodily pleasures, he enjoyed perfect self-control; where pleasures of the mind were concerned, he was insatiable only for men's praise. He was extremely adept at seeing immediately what had to be done when it was not yet obvious, and was exceptionally good at guessing what was likely to happen based on the available evidence; he showed outstanding talent for drawing up, arming, and equipping an army. In raising his soldiers' morale, filling them with good hopes, and dispelling

---

5. Plutarch, *Lives*, 2:147.

> their fear in times of danger by his own fearlessness, he showed himself supremely gifted. All that needed to be done openly he did with the utmost courage, while in situations requiring stealth and speed he also excelled at getting the jump on his enemies before they suspected what was coming. He was utterly reliable in honoring promises and agreements, and no one was less likely to be taken in by deceivers. Uncommonly sparing in the use of money for his own pleasures, he spent ungrudgingly for the benefit of others. If any offense was given by Alexander's sharpness or anger, or if he carried to an extreme his taste for barbarian pomp, I do not myself regard it as a serious matter. One might reasonably take into account Alexander's youth, his uninterrupted good fortune, and the influence of royal counselors who consider what will please, not what will be for the best, and who harm and always will harm the kings they attend. But Alexander is the only ancient king I know of whose nobility moved him to feel remorse for his misdeeds.[6]

Alexander and Themistocles were two of the greatest leaders in the history of the world. But that leadership required that they pay the price of self-sacrifice and hard work. They paid the price physically in that they exercised self-control in terms of bodily pleasures. They paid the price by sacrificing their money and time for the purpose of achieving their goals.

You are never too young to begin paying the price for greatness. Consider the youthful Benjamin Franklin:

> When about 16 years of age I happened to meet with a book, written by one Tryon, recommending a vegetable diet. I determined to go into it. My brother, being yet unmarried, did not keep house, but boarded himself and his apprentices with another family. My refusing to eat flesh occasioned an inconveniency, and I was frequently chid for my singularity. I made myself acquainted with Tryon's manner of preparing some of his dishes, such as boiling potations or, making hasty pudding, and a few others, and then proposed to my brother, that if he would give me, weekly, half the money he paid for my board, I would board myself. He instantly agreed to it, and I presently found that I could save half what he paid me. This was an additional fund for buying books. But I had another advantage in it. My brother and the rest going from the printing-house to their meals, I remained there alone, and, dispatching presently my light repast, which often was no more than a bisket or a slice of bread, a handful of raisins, or a tart from the pastry-cook's and a glass of water, had the rest of the time, till their

---

6. Arrian, *Campaigns of Alexander*, 313.

return, for study, in which I made the greater progress, from that greater clearness of head and quicker apprehension which usually attend temperance in eating and drinking . . . While I was intent on improving my language, I met with an English grammar (I think it was Greenwood's), at the end of which there were two little sketches of the arts of rhetoric and logic, the latter finishing with a specimen of a dispute in the Socratic method, and soon after I procur'd Xenophon's Memorable Things of Socrates, wherein there are many instances of the same method. I was charm'd with it, adopted it, dropt my abrupt contradiction and positive argumentation, and put on the humble inquirer and doubter.[7]

Franklin at sixteen years of age made choices that few young men of that age make. He read great books. He mined wisdom from those books and applied them to his life. At an age when most are spending time playing the games of boys, Franklin was reading the great works of literature and denying himself the lust of the flesh and gluttony. Because he lived like no one else at such a young age, as an adult he achieved greatness.

Another example of a young man who paid the price was Abraham Lincoln. Lincoln was born in poverty, with no formal education, and he found a world open for discovery through reading. A biographer of Lincoln quoted Emily Dickinson, who wrote: "There is no Frigate like a Book to take us Lands away." The biographer applied this to the experience of Lincoln:

> Though the young Lincoln never left the frontier, would never leave America, he traveled with Byron's Childe Harold to Spain and Portugal, the Middle East and Italy; accompanied Robert Burns to Edinburgh; and followed the English kings into battle with Shakespeare. As he explored the wonders of literature and the history of the country, the young Lincoln, already conscious of his own power, developed ambitions far beyond the expectations of his family and neighbors. It was through literature that he was able to transcend his surroundings.[8]

To explore the wonders of literature and history required the young Lincoln to pay the price. He had to sacrifice his time for reading when other boys his age were playing.

To serve the Lord and become a great man or woman in this world requires that you sacrifice those things which do not serve to make you a better person or prepare you for your future. There is nothing that inflames

---

7. Franklin, *Autobiography*, 52–54.
8. Goodwin, *Team of Rivals*, 51.

ambition more, or motivates and excites the mind to great possibilities, than reading. That is why in the Middle Ages the rich and powerful wanted the poor to remain not only poor but also uneducated. If the poor were educated, it would breed ambition and hope for a better life, and that would threaten their control over their lives.

So, pick up and read not only the great works of secular literature, but pick up and read the greatest piece of literature known to man: the Bible, the inspired word of God. When you read the Bible, God moves in your life and transforms your mind through his word. The Spirit of God inspires the reader of God's word to do great things for him.

SACRIFICE

> I beseech you therefore, brethren, by the mercies of God, that you present your bodies a living *sacrifice*, holy, acceptable to God, which is your reasonable service.
> (Rom 12:1)

To achieve greatness in this world requires sacrifice. The sacrifice of the Old Testament was a lifeless and charred body on an altar; the sacrifice of today is a life of devotion, service, purity and holiness. The new life in Christ is the life that has been sacrificed and offered to God. Once we are born again, we cease to live for ourselves; we are under obligation to serve God. Our sacrifice today is to live according to God's will, forsaking the flesh.

Sacrifice means to give up something in order to get something else, or even to be a blessing to someone. God calls us to give up our bodies as a living sacrifice to the Lord. Sacrifice assumes the giving up of something desired. In this case, we are to give up the desires of the flesh. Whether it be sensual pleasures, or greed for money or power, these things are to be sacrificed through the presenting of our bodies to God. We are to yield the desire of our body to God. This is the demand, the cost, and the sacrifice that we are required to pay. The biblical principle of sacrifice carries over to every area of life.

Great achievements require *smart* sacrifice. There are going to be certain activities that you are going to have to say "no" to in order to achieve your dreams. You may even have to give up some good things, things you want, things that you have acquired previously. But, until you sacrifice them, they will be a roadblock to further progress.

Plutarch recorded the military record of Alexander the Great. Alexander was not content with Macedonia or Persia; he had dreams of further conquest into the east:

> Alexander, now intent upon his expedition into India, took notice that his soldiers were so charged with booty that it hindered their marching. Therefore, at break of day, as soon as the baggage waggons were laden, first he set fire to his own, and to those of his friends, and then commanded those to be burnt which belonged to the rest of the army.[9]

In order to achieve his goal, Alexander and his army had to sacrifice the fruits of their previous victories. If there is anything in your life that is hindering your advancement toward achieving your goals, these things must be sacrificed.

As a Christian, the ultimate goal is to become like Christ and attain greatness in his heavenly kingdom. What possessions do you have, what lusts do you have that are keeping you from advancing toward this lofty goal? Whatever it is, sacrifice it, burn it, and you will not miss it. Anything you sacrifice by faith in this world will be returned to you a hundred fold in the kingdom of heaven.

Agis was one of the greatest Spartan kings. As a young man he had to make sacrifices that elevated him to that place in Greek history:

> Agis had been bred very tenderly, in abundance and even in luxury, by his mother Agesistrata and his grandmother Archidamia, who were the wealthiest of the Lacedaemonians, yet, before the age of twenty, he renounced all indulgence in pleasures. Withdrawing himself as far as possible from the gaiety and ornament which seemed becoming to the grace of his person, he made it his pride to appear in the coarse Spartan coat. In his meals, his bathings, and in all his exercises, he followed the old Laconian usage, and was often heard to say, he had no desire for the place of king, if he did not hope by means of that authority to restore their ancient laws and discipline.[10]

In order to become a great king over a warlike people, Agis, from a young age, was willing to sacrifice the wealth and luxury of his family. He denied himself sensual pleasures so that he might restore the former greatness of Sparta.

9. Plutarch, *Lives*, 1:184.
10. Plutarch, *Lives*, 1:320.

To achieve greatness in any endeavor in this world requires a measure of personal sacrifice. We must be willing to sacrifice those desires and activities that would prevent us from achieving our goals. For the Christian, to be great in the kingdom of God requires spiritual sacrifice. Jesus taught us that the greatest of all is the one who is a servant to all. To serve others requires a sacrifice of pride and a willingness to be clothed in humility.

SELF-CONFIDENCE/SENSE OF DESTINY

> For whom He foreknew, He also predestined to be conformed to the image of His Son, that He might be the firstborn among many brethren.
> (Rom 8:29)

One of the key characteristics that sets great men and women apart is this: their confidence is driven by a sense of destiny. For the Christian, they are motivated by a sense of calling and divine purpose. This kind of confidence is reflected in the inspired words of the apostle Paul in Philippians 4:13, "I can do all things through Christ who strengthens me."

A person who believes they are on this earth for a purpose is going to be confident. They will live and work with perseverance, and that purpose will drive them to overcome setbacks and disappointments.

Take young Churchill as an example. He was set up on a blind date with a young, attractive woman. They only went on one date, but years later the woman reflected on her experience with the great Winston Churchill as they were sitting together at a dinner:

> For a long time he remained sunk in abstraction, then he appeared to become suddenly aware of my existence. He turned on me a lowering gaze and asked me abruptly how old I was. I replied that I was nineteen. "And I," he said almost despairingly, "am thirty-two already. Younger than anyone else who counts, though." After a long oration he suddenly ended with the immortal words, "We are all worms, but I do believe I am a glow-worm."[11]

People who do great things in this world are confident. There is a sense of divine purpose that drives them and motivates them to push on and to do their best. If you are a child of God, then you have a great purpose: you are sent to where you are by Jesus for a reason, and you can be assured that

---

11. Gilbert, *Churchill*, 185.

there is something special about you. If we are all worms, then you really are a "glow-worm," reflecting the light of Jesus Christ in a dark world.

It is not about money or about being raised in a healthy home environment, though these help of course. But each of us makes the decision for ourselves. You have all the resources you need to do anything in this world. The question is: will you discover where your true chance of greatness lies and then reach out and seize the opportunity to fulfill it? For Christians, it all ends and begins with the word of God.

To achieve greatness in anything, you have to believe in yourself. You need to have a confidence that comes from the knowledge that you are here for a purpose and that God is directing your paths. You have only one life and your years in this life are not guaranteed. Seize the opportunity that God has given you, and do not let anything in this world keep you from pursuing it.

NEVER QUIT

> And let us not grow weary while doing good, for in due season we
> shall reap if we do not lost heart.
> (Gal 6:9)

There is no one that the world deems great who did not have to face the temptation of giving up. There will always be opposition in any good endeavor. Those who are great are the ones who do not quit, even when facing seemingly insurmountable obstacles. If the goal you are striving after is good and worthy and you have sacrificed to get where you are, nothing should make you turn back.

Pericles gave this powerful advice on achieving greatness:

> Do not betray any sign of being oppressed by your present sufferings, since they whose minds are least sensitive to calamity, and whose hands are most quick to meet it, are the greatest men and the greatest communities.[12]

Those who achieve greatness do not step back from obstacles, but they go and meet them. Even in midst of suffering, do not ever let your demeanor communicate to others that you are near defeat. If God has called

---

12. Thucydides, *Peloponnesian War*, 127.

you to do the work, do not let your mind focus on the difficulties, but in faith and confidence meet your challenges head on and overcome them. The great Greek philosopher Bias once said,

> Be slow to set about an enterprise, but persevere in it steadfastly when once it is undertaken.[13]

This is sage advice from one of the seven great sages of the ancient Greek world. If you set your heart to achieve greatness in life and in the eyes of God, carefully choose the path and the goals for your life. Once those goals are established, never quit. You have only one life to live. Do not waste it: look forward to all the possibilities before you, choose your destiny, and do not let any power, temptation, or influence distract you from your goals.

Above all have a will to win. In the First World War the Germans had attacked France, the lines were set, and thousands of men on both sides were entrenched at the line of battle. The side with the greater will to win would emerge victorious. During these days the French generals debated among themselves on the best military strategy for defeating the Germans. The prevailing theory of the time was "the doctrine of the offensive." Barbara Tuchman, in her classic history of the First World War, described it this way:

> The doctrine of the offensive had its fount in the War College, the ark of the army's intellectual elite, whose director, General Ferdinand Foch, was the molder of French military theory of his time. Foch's mind, like a heart, contained two valves: one pumped spirit into strategy; the other circulated common sense. On the one hand Foch preached a mystique of will expressed in his famous aphorisms, "The will to conquer is the first condition of victory," or more succinctly, "Victoire c'est la volonté," and, "A battle won is a battle in which one will not confess oneself beaten."[14]

If you are to achieve greatness, you must develop a will to win. You will never be victorious over sin or over opposition unless you first set your will to make it happen. There is going to be opposition.

Jesus taught His followers that in this world you will have trouble. Trouble and opposition are realities for all those who set out to achieve some great purpose. Those who determine in their will to never quit will ultimately emerge victorious. During the darkest hours of the Second World

---

13. Diogenes, *Lives of Eminent Philosophers*, 91.
14. Tuchman, *Guns of August*, 32.

War, Winston Churchill modeled what a "never quit" spirit looked like in these words:

> I am having a very rough time now, but look how much better things are than a year ago, when we were alone. We must not lose our faculty to dare, especially in dark days.[15]

In your journey to reaching your destiny, there will be dark days. You must never quit just because there is opposition. It is during those darkest hours that we learn best to trust and rely on God. It is for God to raise us up and to deliver us according to his will. It is for us to go forward in faith, believing in what God has called us to do. Let us decide in our will to never quit, even if it gets us killed. We must never lose our courage to dream great dreams and pursue greatness.

Hector, the prince of Troy, said before he died:

> Tis true I perish, yet I perish great: Yet in a mighty deed I shall expire, Let future ages hear it, and admire.[16]

As Christians we should strive to achieve greatness in the eyes of the Lord. We must never quit, never surrender, and never relent in our willingness to stand for the Lord.

SUBMISSION

> Bondservants, obey in all things your masters according to the flesh, not with eyeservice, as men pleasers, but in sincerity of heart, fearing God.
> (Col 3:22)

When you work for someone else, you have to obey the rules. When you took the position of the job you are presently in, when you were hired and you said "yes," you were saying "yes" to that particular position and all the rules and expectations that came with it.

Now, if over the course of time you find yourself not liking the position you are in, that is not the fault of the employer. That is your problem. You can choose to leave and go find another position. But, as a Christian, you should never disrupt the office through your own dissatisfaction or try

---

15. Churchill, "Hinge of Fate," 228.
16. Polybius, *Histories*, Loc. 5810–15.

to force change that is not warranted by stepping outside and around the company rules.

When you are employed, God's word to you is to obey in all things. And not only that, do it with a good attitude. It is sinful for Christians to act disgruntled and bitter because they think they are not getting the money they deserve or to think they are too good for their job. God's word to employees is to obey in all things, to do your best, and to serve him. If you will choose to do those things, God who reigns over all, who loves you and wants to use you, will bless you in due time. If you are faithful in the small things, God will give you greater things.

Consider Joseph in Potiphar's house. He had been sold into slavery by his brothers. He was reduced to being a household slave in Egypt. Now, Joseph, before being sold into slavery, was a young man with great ambition, and he was a dreamer of great dreams. All that hope vanished when he was sold into slavery.

But Joseph was different: he honored the Lord, worked hard, and obeyed his master in all things. As a result, the Scripture says in Genesis 39:3, "The Lord was with Joseph, and he was a successful man. . . . the Lord made all he did to prosper in his hand." It was from obedience that God's blessing flowed. Ultimately, Joseph went from being a household slave to being the most powerful man under Pharaoh in all of Egypt.

It does not matter where you are right now. What matters is your attitude and choices. If you are unhappy with your present employment, and you have it in your heart to do more, the key is to live in obedience to the rules and the expectations of your present employer. Go over and beyond what is expected where you are right now, and God himself will open up the doors for the future. Diogenes quoted Solon's advice to young men:

> Learn to obey before you command.[17]

The way up is down for a Christian. Jesus said that the greatest among you will be the one who serves all. Be faithful in the small things and faithful where you are now.

In Psalm 78:70–72, the psalmist Asaph wrote about David's calling: "He also chose David his servant and took him from the sheepfolds; from following the ewes that had young He brought him to shepherd Jacob His people, and Israel His inheritance. So he shepherded them according to the integrity of his heart, and guided them by the skillfulness of his hands."

---

17. Diogenes, *Lives of Eminent Philosophers*, 61.

As a king, David led God's people with integrity, just as he did when he was a youth taking care of his father's sheep. It matters how we do the little things and the unimportant things. When we are young, we are tempted to do things halfway. You might think, "What does it matter how I mow this lawn. This is so boring! What does it matter how hard I work on this homework; I just need a C to get out of here. What does it matter how I flip this burger; I cannot stand this boring job anyway and I will not be here long."

But it does matter, because it matters to God! He is watching, and he is looking for character. Our character is defined and established by how well—or how poorly—we do the things that we think are beneath us. When we do the little unimportant and unrecognized things well, God judges us worthy for bigger opportunities. It was because David cared for those sheep that God saw his character; he knew that if David could be a good shepherd of stinky animals, he would be a good and just king for his people Israel. That is a truth that will never change. It is set in stone.

Jesus immortalized this truth in the parable of the talents in Matthew 25:21, "His Lord said to him, well done, good and faithful servant, you were faithful over a few things, I will make you ruler over many things. Enter into the joy of your Lord."

David took care of his sheep with integrity and his character was clearly seen. When he was about to go and fight Goliath, Saul said, "You cannot fight him, you are just a boy." But David said in 1 Samuel 17:35, "Your servant used to keep his father's sheep, and when a lion or a bear came and took a lamb out of the flock, I went out after it and struck it, and delivered the lamb from its mouth; and when it arose against me, I caught it by its beard, and struck and killed it."

David fought a lion and a bear on account of one smelly lamb. What other shepherd would have risked his or her life for one lamb? But David was charged by his father to tend to the sheep and was faithful. God saw David's character and chose him as the man to rule Israel. The ability to submit to authority is a sure sign of future greatness.

WORK HARD

> And whatever you do, do it heartily, as to the Lord and not to men. (Col 3:23)

Paul wrote this passage in the context of first-century slavery, but the principles that he gave apply to the modern workplace. God expects his children to be hard workers and to do their work from the heart, "not with eyeservice, as men pleasers..." (Col. 3:22).

Paul stated they should work "out of soul." Our work, no matter what sort it is, is to be done out of the heart and soul. Work that is only done when the boss is looking is hypocritical and does not please the Lord.

We are all tempted to work a little harder when our superiors are watching, but God's word to the Christian is to work just as hard, whether the boss is present or not. Those who work with their heart and soul are the ones who find advancement. But those who are people-pleasers and work for eye service tend to stay right where they are and then complain: "Why am I always left out? Why do I never get promoted?"

They are passed over because work done under the watchful eye of the boss does not impress near as much as work done when the boss is not watching. When you do your work and your boss comes in and is surprised by how much has been done, that is much more memorable in his or her mind than work done in his or her presence. God's word to employees is not to work as men-pleasers.

Our service is to be with a sincere heart. This high call makes no distinction between pleasant or unpleasant tasks. It simply states that everything must be done energetically, from the heart, whether the boss is present or not. This kind of work pleases God and brings his blessings.

Benjamin Franklin was a hard and diligent worker. Franklin used to say that reading was the only amusement that he allowed himself, but everything else was devoted to work. This practice started in his childhood. Franklin's father used to repeat Proverbs 22:29, "Do you see a man who excels in his work? He will stand before kings; he will not stand before unknown men." In his autobiography Franklin stated:

> I from thence considered industry, as a means of obtaining wealth and distinction, which encouraged me, though I did not think that I should ever literally stand before kings, which, however, has since happened; for I have stood before five, and even had the honor of sitting down with one, the king of Denmark, to dinner.[18]

God's instruction to his children is to work hard.

---

18. Franklin, *Autobiography*, 181.

Achieving Greatness

The Christian is to do their work as though God himself gave the assignment, because, according to the Scripture, that is the truth. God has placed you right where you are, and there is a reason for your present circumstances. If you will, in faith, accept this as truth and work as though God himself called you by name and sent you to that place, God will bless you.

Do not let yourself say, "Oh, I hate my job"; do not be prideful and say, "Oh, I am so much better than this; this job is nothing; I am too good for this." It is not a bad thing to desire to achieve greatness in this world, but if you are to be great, you must be great where you are *now*. Be great in your present situation and if your present employment is not your heart's desire, God will use it as a testing ground and a preparation experience for what is next.

It is like what was called "the little theatre" in ancient Greece named the Odeum of Pericles. The Odeum served for the rehearsal of new comedies as well as tragedies. They were read or repeated without music or decorations. No piece could be presented in the main theatre if it had not been previously approved by judges in the Odeum of Pericles.[19]

We all want to be in the theatre and up on the big stage, with all the music and decorations and all the fame and glory. But before God puts you on the big stage, he first tests you in the Odeum of Pericles. Do your best in the place you are now, follow the company rules, and work where you are now as though God himself gave you the assignment.

Those who work hard will also enjoy peace and joy in their hearts. There is something about knowing that you have put in a full day's work that creates a sense of accomplishment and peace.

Plutarch recorded the history of the Persian invasion of Greece. The Spartans could not believe how lavish and gluttonous the king and people of Persia were. The king of Persia was surrounded with people who catered to his every desire. In comparison, the Spartan king shared in the same day-to-day work and struggles as his soldiers. Plutarch observed:

> Those who labour sleep more sweetly and soundly than those who are laboured for, and could fail to see by comparing the Persians' manner of living with their own that it was the most abject and slavish condition to be voluptuous, but the most noble and royal to undergo pain and labour.[20]

---

19. Gibbon, *Decline and Fall*, 1:41.
20. Plutarch, *Lives*, 1:172.

There is a nobility to honest work, and those who have abundant wealth are often those who are most enslaved by anxiety and depression. As Mark Twain once said:

> A maxim of mine that whenever a man preferred being fed by any other man to starving in independence he ought to be shot.[21]

On one occasion when Twain was in California during the Gold Rush, hoping to make his fortune, he had a friend named Higbie who was struggling to find a job in one of the mines. The following is a long story but well worth reading, for it illustrates what hard work and persistence will accomplish in your life:

> He said, with an outburst of pathetic longing, "If I could only get a job at the Pioneer [a gold mine camp]!"
> I said "What kind of a job do you want at the Pioneer?"
> He said "Why, laborer. They get five dollars a day."
> I said "If that's all you want I can arrange it for you."
> Higbie was astonished. He said "Do you mean to say that you know the foreman there and could get me a job and yet have never said anything about it?"
> "No" I said, "I don't know the foreman."
> "Well" he said, "who is it you know? How is it you can get me the job?"
> "Why," I said, "that's perfectly simple. If you will do as I tell you to do, and don't try to improve on my instructions, you shall have the job before night."
> He said eagerly "I'll obey the instructions, I don't care what they are."
> "Well," I said, "go there and say that you want work as a laborer; that you are tired of being idle; that you are not used to being idle, and can't stand it; that you just merely want the refreshment of work, and require nothing in return."
> He said "Nothing?"
> I said, "That's it—nothing."
> "No wages at all?"
> "No, no wages at all."
> "Not even board?"
> "No, not even board. You are to work for nothing. Make them understand that—that you are perfectly willing to work for nothing. When they look at that figure of yours that foreman will understand that he has drawn a prize. You'll get the job."

21. Twain, *Autobiography*, Loc. 2493-94.

Higbie said indignantly, "Yes, a hell of a job."

I said, "You said you were going to do it, and now you are already criticising. You have said you would obey my instructions. You are always as good as your word. Clear out, now, and get the job."

He said he would.

I was pretty anxious to know what was going to happen—more anxious than I would have wanted him to find out. I preferred to seem entirely confident of the strength of my scheme, and I made good show of that confidence. But really I was very anxious. Yet I believed that I knew enough of human nature to know that a man like Higbie would not be flung out of that place without reflection when he was offering those muscles of his for nothing. The hours dragged along and he didn't return. I began to feel better and better. I began to accumulate confidence. At sundown he did at last arrive and I had the joy of knowing that my invention had been a fine inspiration and was successful.

He said the foreman was so astonished at first that he didn't know how to take hold of the proposition, but that he soon recovered and was evidently very glad that he was able to accommodate Higbie and furnish him the refreshment he was pining for.

Higbie said "How long is this to go on?"

I said "The terms are that you are to stay right there; do your work just as if you were getting the going wages for it. You are never to make any complaint; you are never to indicate that you would like to have wages or board. This will go on one, two, three, four, five, six days, according to the make of that foreman. Some foremen would break down under the strain in a couple of days. There are others who would last a week. It would be difficult to find one who could stand out a whole fortnight without getting ashamed of himself and offering you wages. Now let's suppose that this is a fortnight-foreman. In that case you will not be there a fortnight. Because the men will spread it around that the very ablest laborer in this camp is so fond of work that he is willing and glad to do it without pay. You will be regarded as the latest curiosity. Men will come from the other mills to have a look at you. You could charge admission and get it, but you mustn't do that. Stick to your colors. When the foremen of the other mills cast their eyes upon this bulk of yours and perceive that you are worth two ordinary men they'll offer you half a man's wages. You are not to accept until you report to your foreman. Give him an opportunity to offer you the same. If he doesn't do it then you are free to take up with that other man's offer. Higbie, you'll be foreman of a mine or a mill inside of three weeks, and at the best wages going."

It turned out just so.[22]

Mark Twain gave his friend advice that was worth far more than any gold they could dig out of the mines. Hard work, doing your work as unto the Lord, will lead to blessing. Even if you work for free, it is better to work than to sit around idle and complain about your present job. Go and work! Expect nothing in return, and you will see how God will intervene in your life and open doors that are presently closed.

In his Stoic masterpiece *Meditations*, Marcus Aurelius summed up beautifully how hard work leads to happiness in life:

> If thou workest at that which is before thee, following right reason seriously, vigorously, calmly, without allowing anything else to distract thee, but keeping thy divine part pure, as if thou shouldst be bound to give it back immediately; if thou holdest to this, expecting nothing, fearing nothing, but satisfied with thy present activity according to nature, and with heroic truth in every word and sound which thou utterest, thou wilt live happy. And there is no man who is able to prevent this.[23]

If we desire to achieve greatness in this life, we must strive to work hard. We need to do the work that is before us and do it in the name of the Lord.

---

22. Twain, *Autobiography*, Loc. 13183–229.
23. Aurelius, *Meditations*, Loc. 371–75.

Chapter 4

Things to Avoid

For all that is in the world—the lust of the flesh, the lust of the eyes, and the pride of life—is not of the Father but is of the world. And the world is passing away, and the lust of it; but he who does the will of God abides forever.

(1 John 2:16–17)

If a person desires to lead a virtuous life, there are going to be things he or she needs to avoid. For the Christian, true virtue is found by being in Christ. When a Christian walks in the Spirit, it requires a steadfast commitment to avoid all that is in the world. This includes all the lusts of the world and anything in which Christ himself would not participate. This chapter focuses on the most important things to avoid if you are to live a virtuous life.

VICES

The apostle John says that if a man or woman loves the world or the things in it, the love of God is not in them. As Christians we are to live in the love of God, and we are to carry the love of God to the world.

However, John says if we love the world, the love of God is not in us. This is so important that John spells it out for us in the verse above. What does a parent do when they are warning a child? They bring them close, look them in the eye, and say what needs to be said slowly and clearly.

John speaks to his readers as his spiritual children. He clearly explains what is meant by loving the world: the lust of the flesh, the lust of the eyes, and pride of life. These things are not from God but from the world, from the place where Satan has his throne.

If the vices of this world control you, then you are not controlled by God. The lust of the flesh is a phrase that refers in a general sense to any ungodly desire, specifically physical desires. It refers to someone who is dominated by the vices of their flesh. These vices include such things as gluttony, drug and alcohol addiction, lust, and extravagant living.

The malicious quality of the lust of the flesh is that it can be very subtle and deceptive. It is not just gross immorality, but any thought or behavior that would cause you to neglect God and disregard how others feel. It is the attitude which says, "I am going to do what is best for me. I am going to do what makes me happy no matter what anyone else thinks. I am going to make this choice even though the Bible specifically prohibits it. I am going to do what I want to do."

The lust of the flesh causes its victims to be lazy and indifferent. They become callous towards others. The number one goal of the lust-filled person is to have peace and comfort. They do not want any pressure or responsibility, especially if they do not get something out of it for themselves.

During the reign of Marcus Cato, Rome grew comfortable while enjoying a prolonged period of peace. The people had not been called upon to sacrifice for the state in a long time, and they grew morally dull in their affluence. Noted historian Will Durant described the vices of Rome in this way:

> Equipped with such means, the Roman patriciate and upper middle class passed with impressive speed from stoic simplicity to reckless luxury; the lifetime of Cato (234–149) saw the transformation almost completed. Houses became larger as families became smaller; furniture grew lavish in a race for conspicuous expense; great sums were paid for Babylonian rugs, for couches inlaid with ivory, silver, or gold; precious stones and metals shone on tables and chairs, on the bodies of women, on the harness of horses. As physical exertion diminished and wealth expanded, the old simple diet gave way to long and heavy meals of meat, game, delicacies, and condiments. Exotic foods were indispensable to social position or pretense; one magnate paid a thousand sesterces for the oysters served at a meal; another imported anchovies at 1600 sesterces a cask; another paid

1200 for a jar of caviar. Good chefs fetched enormous prices on the slave auction block. Drinking increased; goblets had to be large and preferably of gold; wine was less diluted, sometimes not at all. Sumptuary laws were passed by the Senate limiting expenditure on banquets and clothing, but as the senators ignored these regulations, no one bothered to observe them.[1]

With such vice and extravagance corrupting Rome and destroying the family unit—which was considered the strength of Roman society—Cato was moved to address the situation. According to Plutarch:

Marcus Cato being once desirous to dissuade the common people of Rome from their selfishness during a time in which the city was being threatened, he began thus to harangue them: "It is a difficult task, O citizens, to make speeches to the belly, which has no ears." Reproving, also, their gluttonous habits, he said it was hard to preserve a city where a fish sold for more than an ox.[2]

The people had fallen in love with pleasure. The lust of the flesh refers to physical sin, but the lust of the eyes is inward and refers to covetousness. We are not to allow a spirit of covetousness to dominate us. The tenth commandment says, "You shall not covet."

The eyes are the gateway to the heart and soul. If we allow our eyes to look longingly and lustfully on the things of this world, it causes us to be ruled by evil thoughts and not the Spirit of God. When a person is given over to the lust of the eyes and coveting what others have, he or she will have no peace and satisfaction.

Paul revealed the antidote to the lust of the eyes in Philippians 4:11, "I have learned in whatever state I am to be content." If I am prosperous, or if I am persecuted and unfairly treated, I am to be content in the Lord. But, those who are ruled by the lust of the eyes do not want to do without. They are not on a mission for the Lord. They are on the hunt in this world to heap upon themselves all they can get.

If we focus our eyes on heaven, and on Christ and his word, our hope will not be in this world. This focus will cause us to be profitable to the Lord. If what you live for in this world is Christ, then nothing else in the world will cause you to look at it and lust after it. The more vices control us, the more we lust for what we can acquire in this world and the less willing we are to part with it.

1. Durant, "Caesar and Christ," 88.
2. Plutarch, *Lives*, 2:462.

The more material things we amass, the more fear we will have of losing them. Plutarch related a story from the reign of the Greek Antigonus. In the army of Antigonus, a particular soldier was unmatched in his battlefield heroics. The man was utterly fearless. The only negative thing about him was that he was in poor health and had a weak constitution. Antigonus asked him why he was always sick and discovered that the man had a disease.

Antigonus commanded his physicians to employ all their skill, and if possible, to heal him. This they did and with great success. However, once the brave hero was cured, he never again would put himself in danger or be aggressive on the battlefield. Antigonus grew angry with him because of his change and demanded to know why he no longer showed himself brave in battle. The man stated the cause:

> Sir, you are the cause of my cowardice. You freed me from those miseries which made me care little for life.[3]

When a man has hope for worldly life and success, it causes him to be less willing to sacrifice for others. That is the lust of the eyes. It is more than just sexual temptation.

The lust of the eyes refers to one who desires the things of this world more than the things of God. The eyes are the windows of possibilities. When we see the possibility of great wealth, we see the possibility of gratifying our flesh, and we chase it. Just as that soldier lost his bravery when he was healed from his disease and suddenly realized that he could have a long and prosperous life, those who live dominated by the lust of the eyes will always be spiritual cowards. When our worldly expectations outweigh our eternal hope, we lose our faith and spiritual courage.

The Christian is not to use worldly eyes, but spiritual eyes. All of the vices that feed our flesh will cause harm and cause us to miss God's best for our lives. In that light, Thomas Paine once noted:

> An association of vices will reduce us more than the sword.[4]

The remaining sections in this chapter on things to avoid could accurately be labeled vices. If any of these begin to work their way into your life, it will be more dangerous than a sword.

---

3. Plutarch, *Lives*, 2:385.
4. Paine, *Collected Writings*, 232.

BLIND IGNORANCE

> Let them alone. They are *blind* leaders of the blind. And if the blind leads the blind, both will fall into a ditch.
> (Matt 15:14)

Blind ignorance occurs when people believe everything they hear and become dogmatic about things that they have not fully tested. This is one of the primary pitfalls of being immature. To avoid this, you must not believe everything you hear, and you must make sure you truly understand everything you believe. Those who are ruled by blind ignorance are led into foolishness. Winston Churchill noted this among the youth of England in the years prior to the start of the Second World War:

> In 1933, the students of the Oxford Union, under the inspiration of a Mr. Joad, passed their ever-shameful resolution, "That this House refuses to fight for King and country." It was easy to laugh off such an episode in England, but in Germany, in Russia, in Italy, in Japan, the idea of a decadent, degenerate Britain took deep root and swayed many calculations. Little did the foolish boys who passed the resolution dream that they were destined quite soon to conquer or fall gloriously in the ensuing war, and prove themselves the finest generation ever bred in Britain. Less excuse can be found for their elders, who had no chance of self-repudiation in action. I cannot resist telling this story. The Oxford Union invited me to address them. I declined to do so, but said I would give them an hour to ask me questions. One of the questions was, "Do you think Germany was guilty of making the last war?" I said, "Yes, of course." A young German Rhodes scholar rose from his place and said, "After this insult to my country I will not remain here." He then stalked out amid roars of applause. I thought him a spirited boy. Two years later it was found out in Germany that he had a Jewish ancestor. This ended his career in Germany.[5]

The young German man in this story was not willing to accept established historical fact due to his blind ignorance. This is truly a thing to avoid.

Blind ignorance is closely associated with unreasonableness. Those who act and speak without the ability to reason soundly exist in a dangerous state of being. When a society falls into this state, history proves that

---

5. Churchill, "Gathering Storm," 85.

Seeking Virtue

evil is the result. Epictetus describes what such a state of being looks like on an individual level:

> Now there are two kinds of petrifaction: one is the petrifaction of the intellect, the other of the sense of shame, when a man stands in array, prepared neither to assent to manifest truths nor to leave the fighting line.[6]

The word "petrifaction" simply means "petrified." Spiritually, it refers to a state of hardness or hard-heartedness. It means that a person has fallen into a state of blindness and is unable to use sound reason and discernment. It is a sad state when a person is petrified in his or her intellect. They become so locked down in assumptions that they are no longer willing to listen to reason.

But a worse state is when they are petrified in their sense of shame. At that point, they are so lost in the lies they have believed that they will not recognize clear truth, nor will they cease arguing for their error. They are petrified in ignorance. Jesus said of such people, "Do not throw your pearls before swine" (Matt 7:6).

BURNOUT

> Come aside by yourselves to a deserted place and rest a while.
> (Mark 6:31)

Many of the stories related in this book have to do with hard work and self-denial. Truly, you will not go far without those characteristics. However, you must also guard against burnout. Our purpose in life is serious, but God would also have us joyful and happy. You must take time for leisure and avoid working all the time. If you do not, you will burn out and thus will not be able to achieve your goals.

Herodotus shared the habits of Amasis, a great Egyptian leader who worked hard but did not neglect his need for rest:

> Amasis established the following daily routine for himself. He worked diligently on serious matters of government from dawn until the peak market hour, but after that he would banter with his ... companions. His close friends and family were disturbed by this behavior and admonished him: "Sire, you are not conducting

---

6. Epictetus, *Discourses*, 1:37.

yourself properly by pursuing worthless pastimes. You ought to be seated solemnly upon your stately throne, transacting affairs of state throughout the day; that way, the Egyptians would know that they were being governed by a competent man, and your reputation would improve. But as it is, you are not acting at all like a king." Amasis retorted: "When archers need to use their bows, they string them tightly, but when they have finished using them, they relax them. For if a bow remained tightly strung all the time, it would snap and be of no use when someone needed it. The same principle applies to the daily routine of a human being: if someone wants to work seriously all the time and not let himself ease off for his share of play, he will go insane without ever knowing it, or at the least suffer a stroke. And it is because I recognize this maxim that I allot a share of my time to each aspect of life." That is how Amasis answered them.[7]

Burnout is not specifically a vice, but it is a state of being that is often caused by vice. Pride, lust of the flesh, and greed are vices that cause people to overwork and to hide their true condition to others, and the result is often burnout. No matter what line of work you are in, burnout is to be avoided. Do not be like the bow of Amasis, strung so tight and never relieved through relaxation until it is too late and then . . . "snap!"

ENVY

The apostle Paul wrote in 1 Corinthians 13:4, "Love does not envy." Jealousy and envy are especially ugly in the life of a Christian. Jealousy means that you want something someone else has. Even more detestable is the kind of envy that says, "I wish they did not have what they have." Do you ever have that thought creep into your heart? If you do, repent, because that is far from love. Love does not envy.

We need to come to the place in our lives where we can truly be happy when we see others blessed. We need to be able to hug someone who has just received a promotion or who is excited about a blessing in their life, even if our lives are filled with disappointment at the moment.

The ability to rejoice with others is an act of love. How can God, who sees all, not help but smile upon you when he sees you being happy for someone else, even when you are not where you want to be?

---

7. Herodotus, *Histories*, 199.

Seeking Virtue

Jonathan, the best friend of David, is the perfect example of a love that does not envy. He willingly sacrificed the throne of Israel to David because he knew that God had chosen David as king. That is love, to give up power and glory to another and do it willingly. Love does not envy. Envy will act as rottenness to your bones. Avoid it at all costs. The Roman Pliny once said:

> One may be sure a man has many virtues if he admires those of others.[8]

Never allow yourself to sit around and stew over the success of others. Envy will cause you to secretly wish for their failure, and God does not bless such a heart. You know you are spiritually healthy when you can admire virtue in others.

At the same time, do not be disturbed by the envy or jealousy of others directed toward you. You will feel the sting of backbiting, but let the Lord fight those battles. They are not for you.

Suetonius related an occasion when Tiberius became enraged because he discovered a harsh letter written about Caesar Augustus. Tiberius informed the emperor of the man who wrote the letter and desired him to be punished. Augustus wisely stated:

> My dear Tiberius, do not be carried away by the ardor of youth in this matter, or take it too much to heart that anyone speak evil of me; we must be content if we can stop anyone from doing evil to us.[9]

Envy causes a person to desire another's possessions or worse, to hope that others will fail in order to help him or her succeed. Someone once wrote, "Envy spies out blemishes, that she may lower another by defeat."[10] Envy is insidious because it causes a person to sin and desire the destruction of others. The envious never recognize this destructive vice in themselves. Others might see it in them, but they cannot.

How do you know if you are envious? Do you fantasize about others failing? Is there someone that you know is attempting to do good, a fellow believer or an honest coworker, and you find yourself taking pleasure in the thought of them failing? Do you fantasize about them falling on their face so that you can get ahead or feel better about yourself? That is envy, and it has no place in the heart of God's child. Bitter envy is a great sin.

---

8. Durant, *Caesar and Christ*, 440.
9. Suetonius, *Lives of the Caesars*, 77.
10. Charles Caleb Colton, unknown source.

An envious and self-seeking spirit causes an even greater evil to be close by: hypocrisy. A hypocrite is a playactor. They see someone else doing something great and they want that attention and glory for themselves, so they act like something they are not. They are self-seeking and act a certain way on the outside, but it does not come from their heart. They want the glory or attention, but without the sacrifice. Jesus rebuked the Pharisees in Matthew 23:28: "Even so you outwardly appear righteous to men, but inside you are full of hypocrisy and lawlessness."

Cicero, the great Roman statesman, was revered and famous in his day. He said this of himself:

> This course of life perhaps offends those who fix their eyes on the glitter and show of my professional position, but are unable to appreciate its anxieties and laboriousness.[11]

In his wisdom, Cicero called out the envious for their hypocrisy. They saw his glory and the public praise he received, and many pretenders—inspired by all the public praise—rose up in imitation of him. But they did so without counting the cost and failed to appreciate all the anxieties and hard work that came with his public position. Cicero served the public from the heart, from a sense of duty and at great personal cost. Hypocrites just want the public praise.

This was the failing of Annanias and Saphira in the book of Acts. They saw the public praise poured on Barnabas when he sold all his property and laid it all at the apostles' feet. Barnabas gave up all he had and lived to build the church; he did that from the heart, and it was the calling of God on his life.

Annanias and Saphira sold their property and only gave a portion of the proceeds, but lied about it and said they gave it all. They lied to the church and died in judgment for their hypocrisy. For two thousand years, they have served as a warning to all pretenders. Do not let envy turn into hypocrisy. Where there is envy and self-seeking, every evil thing is there.

GREED

> He who loves silver will not be satisfied with silver; nor he who loves abundance, with increase. This also is vanity.
> (Eccl 5:10)

11. Cicero, *Letters*, 130.

This is how the world thinks: "If I were wealthy, then I would be happy. If I could just get this much money in the bank, then I would be satisfied." That is what we are tempted to think, but according to Solomon the acquisition of silver does not give satisfaction to the soul. Worldly abundance does not satisfy spiritual desires. Those who make themselves slaves to the world are working for things that will never satisfy.

Isaiah 55:2 says, "Why do you spend money for what is not bread, and your wages for what does not satisfy? Listen carefully to me, and eat what is good, and let your soul delight itself in abundance." God tells us to listen to him, trust him, and believe in him. He speaks to us as his children and says, "Why are you, my child, living to be rich, when I have told you not to love money?"

Understand there is nothing wrong with success and wealth, unless it becomes our god! This is not a warning only for those who are rich; there are just as many poor people who are greedy and being consumed with the desire for more and more. What we decide to live for is a choice we make, because our nature is to be greedy and never satisfied. The greedy invest a small sum of money, and if it turns into a great sum of money, are they satisfied? No, what they do is take the great sum of money and try to turn it into a vast sum of money. The famous Roman poet Ovid wrote of rich men:

> Both their wealth and a furious lust of wealth increase, and when they possess the most they seek for more.[12]

It is human nature to be greedy and never be satisfied. Several years ago, I took my family to Disney World, and we went to all the parks. The greatest theme parks in the history of mankind, and we were there! Then we got in our minivan to head home and not two hours had passed when one of my young sons was bored and he said, "Daddy!" I said, "Yes my son," and I was thinking, "Oh he is going to say thank you, he is going to sigh and say how satisfied he is with four days of fun." But no, he said, "Daddy, when can we go to Chuck E. Cheese?"

It is human nature to be greedy. God says to his children, "Why will you not listen to me? Why do you live seeking satisfaction in wealth? Do you not know that it will never satisfy?" God warns us to not live greedy lives. God spoke through Ezekiel the prophet concerning all those who spend their lives in greed and selfishness: "They will throw their silver into

---

12. Ovid, *Fasti*, 1.

the streets, and their gold will be like refuse; their silver and their gold will not be able to deliver them in the day of the wrath of the Lord" (Ezek 7:19).

W. A. Criswell told the following story in a sermon from the time when he was a young preacher leading a revival in East Texas. After the morning service, he went to the home of a couple in the church for lunch. As they were waiting for the lunch to be prepared, he sat on the front porch with the husband. Criswell described the conversation that followed this way:

> And, as we sat there, he pointed to a vast sea of oil derricks. When they brought in that oil field in East Texas, each one of those derricks represented a flow, a gusher, of ten thousand barrels a day. And, as he pointed out to me that great mass of derricks, he also pointed out to me that his fence line in the sloping of the hill on which his home was built, that to the fence line of his property, there was not a derrick standing. And the farmer said to me: "Preacher, when they were bringing in those oil wells—and coming up, and coming up, and coming up to my fence line, I was expecting those gushers on my farm. And he said: "In the strange providence of God, when they got to my fence line down there, the holes were dry, not a drop of oil." And he said: "I felt the judgment of God on me. All of my neighbors immensely wealthy and I on this farm of poverty." Then he says: "Then as the days passed, all of those families down there broke up in separation and divorce, every one of them." He said: "There's not a family down there that stayed together in their wealth and in their riches; their homes broke up in bitterness, and hatred, and separation." And he said: "Preacher, my wife and my children are still here." And he said: "I have decided that the best thing God ever did for me was when He stopped that oil flow at that barbed wire fence that separates my farm from those derricks."[13]

Those who strive for wealth do not realize the danger that comes with prosperity. Solomon says that money will not buy happiness. Greed is a vice to avoid at all costs.

DISLOYALTY

> I see the treacherous, and am disgusted, because they do not keep your word.
> (Ps 119:158)

13. Criswell, "Rich Man and God."

A disloyal person has a self-serving motive in everything they do, and it is very unattractive. When a friend, a church, or an employer is generous and faithful to you, never "return the favor" by being disloyal. Even if you find yourself in a situation where you feel it is justified, it is dangerous to engage in an act of betrayal. Unless the one you are betraying is an evil tyrant who is harming other people, disloyalty will only give you a bad name. Consider this story from Herodotus:

> After Artabazos had taken Olynthos, he ambitiously turned his thoughts to Poteidaia, and as he did, he found that Timoxeinos, the general of the Skionaians, was more than willing to arrange for the betrayal of the place to him. How this started, I cannot say, since no one speaks of this. But in the end it happened like this. Timoxeinos would write a letter to Artabazos, or Artabazos would write one to him, and they would wrap the message around an arrow beneath the point, tie it to the feathers, then shoot it to an agreed-upon place. But the plan of Timoxeinos to betray Poteidaia was detected, for on one occasion when Artabazos shot an arrow to the assigned location, he missed his aim and hit a man of Poteidaia in the shoulder instead. A crowd of people gathered around this wounded man, as tends to happen in war; they at once pulled out the arrow, and when they perceived the letter, they brought it to their generals.[14]

Herodotus then explains how, after they read the letter attached to the arrow, everyone in the city learned that Timoxeinos had conspired to betray them. The "aim" of disloyal people is never on target; avoid them at all costs.

PRIDE

> *Pride* goes before destruction, and a haughty spirit before a fall.
> (Prov 16:18)

This is a verse every believer needs to know by heart, "Pride goes before destruction, and a haughty spirit before a fall." And the next verse goes along with it: "Better to be of a humble spirit with the lowly, than to divide the spoil with the proud."

This is a promise from God's word to believers: pride and a haughty spirit lead to a fall; they remove God's hand of protection and blessing.

---

14. Herodotus, *Histories*, 654.

Solomon even says it is better to surround ourselves with the lowly of this world than it is to hang around with the super successful. Why is it better? Because God does not look kindly upon the proud. In fact, God opposes the proud. He lists pride as one of the things that he hates. Proverbs 8:13 says, "Pride and arrogance and the evil way and the perverse mouth I hate." God even gives a special name for the proud in Proverbs 21:24: "A proud and haughty man—"scoffer" is his name; he acts with arrogant pride." God calls the proud and haughty by the name of "scoffer." A scoffer is a derider, and one who scorns and ridicules.

These are not characteristics you want present in your life. Are you a scoffer? Are you one who goes around ridiculing others, scorning others, always criticizing, and looking for the bad in everyone else? This is pride, and it will lead to a fall.

In its essence, pride is thinking more highly of ourselves than we ought. When we are prone to criticizing others rather than just focusing on ourselves and our own work, it is pride. This is dangerous because, instead of acknowledging that everything that we are and the abilities that we have come from God and his grace, we are claiming all the glory for ourselves.

Pride can also cause harm to others. Psalm 10:2 says, "The wicked in his pride persecutes the poor; let them be caught in the plots which they have devised." Add to that Psalm 73:6, "Therefore pride serves as their necklace; violence covers them like a garment." When we give place to pride in our hearts, it always leads to violence.

Pride is unforgiving and unyielding, and it keeps us from reconciling with a brother in the Lord. The psalmist says that pride causes us to clothe ourselves in violence. It is like a necklace that hangs around the neck. When a man lets his pride get out of control, he cannot forget a wrong done to him. If he has done wrong, a prideful man cannot simply say, "I'm sorry, I should not have done that." Instead he hangs that necklace around his neck, and he seeks to get even and to destroy the one that he is against. What else would cause a man or woman to hang onto bitterness, refuse reconciliation, constantly live with an edge about them, and always scheme to get even or to embarrass others? Nothing satisfies them because they have hung pride around their neck like a necklace.

In the old days, pride often led to duels. Even in America, dueling was not uncommon. Someone would offend someone else, and the next thing you know, the two men would have pistols in their hands shooting at each other. If a man was challenged to a duel and refused to accept the challenge,

Seeking Virtue

his pride would not allow him to live with himself. As a result, such pride caused pain and suffering for many.

Alexander Hamilton, one of the most brilliant men of colonial America, was the first secretary of the treasury under George Washington. He was the man who, through the Federalist Papers, helped to create the constitutional government of America. Hamilton was killed in a duel by Vice President Aaron Burr. That streak of pride lies in all men. They will do wrong rather than lose face. Hamilton was a Christian, with young children still at home, and he loved his family. He went off to duel Burr, and when it was his turn to shoot, he shot over the head of Burr on purpose. This was the gentlemanly thing to do in a duel. But Burr, in his fierce anger and pride, took dead aim and shot Hamilton.

Hamilton did not die right away but was taken home near death. His seven children came before him, but he waved them off because the grief was too much to bear.

Pride causes harm to others. Burr's pride caused the death of Hamilton. Hamilton's pride caused his wife to be left a widow and his children to be raised without a father.[15] This is why Psalm 16:19 says, "Better to be of a humble spirit with the lowly, than to divide the spoil with the proud." Pride does nothing but cause harm to ourselves and everyone around us.

Pride has been called the "arch-sin." In a very real sense, pride is the root sin from which all others flow. Pride is self-seeking and self-serving. Pride exalts self. Pride is a sin against the first Commandment, "you shall have no other gods before Me." God is to have the primary place in your heart. He alone should reign over your heart. But in pride, most people choose to love self and to serve self above everything and everyone, including God.

Solomon tells us the inevitable result in Proverbs 29:23, "A man's pride will bring him low." King Nebuchadnezzar of Babylon is the ultimate example of this truth. Daniel had warned Nebuchadnezzar that God was watching him and judging his heart. He warned him to give up pride. One evening, Nebuchadnezzar looked out over that great city and, with pride in his heart, exalted himself and said: "Look at what I have done." And in an instant, God's judgment fell and Nebuchadnezzar lost his mind and for seven years lived as a madman with the wild animals.

Whatever is considered great in this world is nothing to God. To exalt yourself rather than God will always lead to destruction. We all learned the

---

15. Chernow, *Alexander Hamilton*, 695–709.

nursery rhyme "Humpty Dumpty" when we were kids. That story is about pride: "Humpty Dumpty sat on a wall, Humpty Dumpty had a great fall. All the king's horses, and all the king's men could not put Humpty Dumpty together again."

Most of us think Humpty Dumpty was an obese egg who fell off a wall. Actually, Humpty Dumpty was a large cannon used during the English Civil War in the seventeenth century. The cannon protected a walled fortress. It was placed high on the walls, and the soldiers called it Humpty Dumpty. With that large cannon, they thought they were secure and would have no problem defending the city. As the city was being attacked, the wall beneath Humpty Dumpty took a direct hit and caused it to fall to the ground. All the king's men and all the king's horses tried to get Humpty Dumpty working again, but failed.

All of us build walls of protection around our lives. Are you humbly trusting God to be your wall of protection, or is your life being protected by the uncertain "humpty dumpties" of this world? Trusting in the things of this world cannot give security. They do not give peace and assurance. Symon Patrick once wrote,

A proud man and a covetous are never at rest.[16]

Why can they never rest? Because nothing in this world is certain. Trust in the Lord, God said in Isaiah 66:2–3, "Heaven is My throne, and earth is My footstool. Where is the house that you will build Me? For all those things My hand has made, and all those things exist, says the Lord. But on this one will I look. On him who is poor and of a contrite spirit, and who trembles at My word."

God loves those who love his word, but he hates pride. Psalm 31:23 says, "Oh, love the Lord all you his saints! For the Lord preserves the faithful, and fully repays the proud person." God, through his word, has promised us that when the proud wrong their fellow man, they will be repaid by God himself. If you, in your pride, cause harm to others, the Lord will fully repay you. What goes around comes around. All of us who are Christians have Christ as the foundation of our lives, and we are all building on that foundation. Through the choices we make and the words we speak, we are all erecting a structure on that foundation which will one day be judged by fire.

---

16. Patrick, *Heart's Ease*, 61.

Seeking Virtue

Pride causes us to build up monuments to ourselves rather than to God. When we build monuments to ourselves rather to God, it will come back to haunt us.

Just before the beginning of the Revolutionary War, King George III of England celebrated the repeal of the Stamp Act by erecting a gilded lead statue of himself sitting on a colossal horse dressed as a Roman emperor. He had it placed at Bowling Green overlooking the Hudson River in New York City. It was a monument built for his own vanity. When the war started and the Declaration of Independence was read, the soldiers and townspeople gathered at Bowling Green and pulled down the beautiful statue, removing the head of the king.

The lead statue weighed four thousand pounds. It was loaded up and sent to Litchfield, Connecticut, where it was melted down to make 42,088 musket balls. Reportedly, "One wit predicted that the king's soldiers will probably have melted majesty fired at them."[17]

The king erected a statue in pride, but he was repaid in full. Pride always backfires. And, spiritually, the same will happen to anyone who erects a monument to themselves. God fully repays the proud.

Pride is a sin that causes others to lose respect for you, and if you are not careful it will lead to choices that put you into embarrassing situations. Plutarch related the story of a great battle that was set to take place near Athens. The Athenian general, Phocion, was leading the armies of Athens. He was renowned for his leadership and his ability to win battles. He arranged his soldiers on the battlefield, gave his orders, and was awaiting the advance of the enemy:

> Afterwards, having formed the battle, one who wished to show his bravery advanced out of his post before the rest, but on the enemy's approaching, lost heart, and retired back into his rank. "Young man," said Phocion, "are you not ashamed twice in one day to desert your station, first that on which I had placed you, and secondly that on which you had placed yourself?"[18]

Pride will make you look foolish and it can also make you look selfish. General Ulysses S. Grant once said:

---

17. Chernow, *Alexander Hamilton*, 77.
18. Plutarch, *Lives*, 1:261.

> The worst excuse a soldier can make for declining service is that he once ranked the commander he is ordered to report to.[19]

Grant had an entire army to run and an enemy to face; when he gave an order he expected it to be obeyed quickly and without question. When he filled positions with men and assigned rank, he needed it to be done efficiently and expected everyone to do their job. The last thing Grant needed was someone filled with petty pride to decline an assignment because someone that once ranked under him would now be ranked above him. That is foolish pride.

The day may come when someone less deserving is promoted above you. Always remember this: it is not going to help your cause if you react pridefully and are perceived as not being a team player. It is far better to do the work that you have to do and show nothing but respect and support to those above you. Avoid pride and the Lord will promote you in due time.

DWELLING ON THE PAST

> No one, having put his hand to the plow, and looking back, is fit
> for the kingdom of God.
> (Luke 9:62)

We must avoid dwelling on the past. Those who are haunted by past hurts and offenses rarely are able to function well in the present. In the face of a looming German invasion, Churchill, Roosevelt, and other political leaders were tempted to cast blame on the failure to stop Hitler sooner. Churchill was wise enough to know that dwelling on the past could do nothing but cause division among the Allies, and he stated:

> Of this I am certain, that if we open a quarrel between the past and
> the present, we shall find that we have lost the future.[20]

This was a principle that guided Churchill and served him well, enabling him to overlook past slights that could have distracted him from dealing with the problems he was currently facing. Always avoid dwelling on the past, which serves no purpose but to cause division and hurt feelings. Dwelling on the past is a sign of an unforgiving heart.

---

19. Grant, *Memoirs*, 369.
20. Meacham, *Franklin and Winston*, 30.

Seeking Virtue

LUST

> For all that is in the world—the lust of the flesh, the lust of the eyes, and the pride of life—is not of the Father but is of the world.
> (1 John 2:16)

There are many forms of lust. Some lust after power; others lust after money and other material things. But the most common and dangerous form of lust is sexual lust. An uncontrolled sexual appetite will destroy a person and disconnect them from God. God is holy and if we are his children, he lives within us. Paul said of Christians in 1 Corinthians 6:19 that our bodies are temples of the Holy Spirit. It is dangerous for a child of God to engage in sexual sins.

In a passage in which he sounds more like the apostle Paul than a Greek philosopher, Epictetus argued that our motivation for avoiding lust is because we are "fragments of God":

> But you are a being of primary importance; you are a fragment of God; you have within you a part of Him. Why, then, are you ignorant of your own kinship? Why do you not know the source from which you have sprung? Will you not bear in mind, whenever you eat, who you are that eat, and whom you are nourishing? Whenever you indulge in intercourse with women, who you are that do this? Whenever you mix in society, whenever you take physical exercise, whenever you converse, do you not know that you are nourishing God, exercising God? You are bearing God about with you, you poor wretch, and know it not! Do you suppose I am speaking of some external God, made of silver or gold? It is within yourself that you bear Him, and do not perceive that you are defiling Him with impure thoughts and filthy actions. Yet in the presence of even an image of God you would not dare to do anything of the things you are now doing. But when God Himself is present within you, seeing and hearing everything, are you not ashamed to be thinking and doing such things as these, O insensible of your own nature, and object of God's wrath![21]

In a similar way, Cicero, the Roman statesman, accurately portrayed the danger of lust and why it must be avoided:

> No more deadly curse than sensual pleasure has been inflicted on mankind by nature, to gratify which our wanton appetites are

---

21. Epictetus, *Discourses*, 1:255.

roused beyond all prudence or restraint. It is a fruitful source of treasons, revolutions, secret communications with the enemy. In fact, there is no crime, no evil deed, to which the appetite for sensual pleasures does not impel us. Fornications and adulteries, and every abomination of that kind, are brought about by the enticements of pleasure and by them alone. Intellect is the best gift of nature or God: to this divine gift and endowment there is nothing so inimical as pleasure. For when appetite is our master, there is no place for self-control; nor where pleasure reigns supreme can virtue hold its ground. To see this more vividly, imagine a man excited to the highest conceivable pitch of sensual pleasure. It can be doubtful to no one that such a person, so long as he is under the influence of such excitation of the senses, will be unable to use to any purpose either intellect, reason, or thought. Therefore nothing can be so execrable and so fatal as pleasure; since, when more than ordinarily violent and lasting, it darkens all the light of the soul.[22]

In the age in which we live, where sexual images are so easily and privately attained on our phones and computers, there are many dark souls who are addicted to lust. Modern technology has caused us to enter into a spiritual "dark age." Lust works in degrees: once we give into it just a little bit, if not quickly cut out of our lives, the flesh takes over and, before long, one can be completely mastered by the lust of the flesh. We all know how this sin works. We know how the devil attacks us with temptation. When we give in to some temptation or sin, we say, "I will not do it again, I will overcome." But then we do it again and again, until at some point, we become so engrossed in it, we feel as though there is no way to overcome. For some, they grow so weak that they start forgetting that it is wrong and justify the behavior. Epictetus warns:

> But if you be once defeated and say that by and by you will overcome, and then a second time do the same thing, know that at last you will be in so wretched a state and so weak that by and by you will not so much as notice that you are doing wrong, but you will even begin to offer arguments in justification of your conduct; and then you will confirm the truth of the saying of Hesiod: "Forever with misfortunes dire must he who loiters cope."[23]

If you loiter in sin and live a sinful lifestyle, the misfortunes will come and you will have to cope with them. What we need to do is fight the good

---

22. Cicero, *Letters*, 60.
23. Epictetus, *Discourses*, 1:349.

fight; we are in a spiritual battle. Pray like David in Psalm 31:4, "Pull me out of the net which they have secretly laid for me, for You are my strength."

The eyes not only lust after sensual things, but material things as well. The lust of the eyes for the things of this world is something that you must strive to avoid. When someone lets themselves lust after the world, it causes them to forget virtue and desire luxury. This is the aim of temptation: the evil one who opposes us will tempt us to look at what others have and strongly desire it. When such desire is born into our hearts, we will even be tempted to compromise our faith in order to fulfill those desires.

Valerius Maximus gave us a powerful example of how the leaders of Sparta constantly wanted to keep their people from looking at the lifestyle of the Persians. In the following quote the word "Asia" refers to Persia:

> The state of Sparta was very close to our ancestors in its austerity, and it held the same principles as they did. In keeping with the very strict laws of Lycurgus, the state for a long time prevented its citizens from looking to Asia, because they might be captivated by its enticements and fall into a decadent way of life. The Spartans had heard that luxury and excessive spending and all kinds of unnecessary pleasures derived from that place, and that the Ionians were the first to invent the custom of wearing perfume and garlands at parties and having dessert afterward, which are significant incitements to decadence. The Spartans took pleasure in hard work and endurance, so it is not at all surprising that they did not want the firm muscles of their country to be made soft and weak by the corruption of foreign pleasures. They saw that it was much easier to move from virtue to decadence than from decadence to virtue. Their own leader, Pausanias, showed that their fears were not unfounded. He had performed the greatest deeds, but as soon as he gave himself up to the ways of Asia, he lost all shame and his courage was undermined by the effeminate lifestyle of that place.[24]

There is nothing more tragic than when a brother or sister in Christ, whom we love and respect, falls away from the Lord and is corrupted by the lust of the eyes. The corruption of the good is always the worst form of corruption. There is a famous Latin phrase which translated says, "Corruption in the best is the worst corruption." Christians are commanded to do good and are to be known for their faithfulness to the Lord. When a Christian is corrupted by sin, it is the worst form of corruption.

---

24. Maximus, *Memorable Deeds and Sayings*, 56–57.

William Shakespeare expressed this in "Sonnet 94": "For the fairest things grow foulest by foul deeds; / lilies that fester smell far worse than weeds." And that is our experience: those that we admire, whom we love and highly esteem, hurt us the most when they become corrupt and live selfishly and sinfully.

AN UNCONTROLLED TONGUE

> And the *tongue* is a fire, a world of iniquity . . . and it is set on fire by hell.
> (Jas 3:6)

If I were to ask what is the most destructive weapon in the world, most would immediately think of nuclear weapons or other weapons of mass destruction. Indeed a nuclear weapon in the hands of a terrorist would be a volatile and dangerous threat. Fortunately, that has not happened yet and very few people in the world have access to these weapons.

However, there is another weapon to which every human on earth has access. Every one of us carries this weapon with us everywhere we go. The potential for destruction with this weapon is so great that James 3 tells us that it "sets on fire the course of nature, and it is set on fire by hell."

What is this incredibly powerful weapon that we all possess and carry with us? According the Bible, it is our tongues. Your tongue is a weapon which possesses great power and can be used to destroy and hurt. However, if it is restrained, it can be used to bless and to build. To be virtuous you must avoid an uncontrolled tongue.

James says the source of evil words is the fires of hell. He could not state it any stronger than that: nothing in this world can relate to the fires of hell except our words. Indeed, one man's tongue can change world history. Consider the words of Adolph Hitler. Beginning with his words, Hitler decimated continents. He recorded his evil words in his book *Mein Kampf*, and he spoke them in his speeches. Someone has estimated that for every word of *Mein Kampf*, over two hundred people died.

Yes, the evil tongue is set on fire by hell, but, through God, the tongue may also be set on fire from heaven as well! A kind word to a young child; a husband whispering a kind word to his wife; a word of affirmation to a person can set him or her on a course to peace and even greatness.

A word from the tongue of a passionate believer or preacher can bring conviction to kings. It is said that Mary Queen of Scots said of the great John Knox, "I fear his tongue more than an army of 10,000 men." We need to make sure our tongues are converted along with our souls.

The tongue can lead us into many types of sinful behaviors, the most common of which is gossip. You will have times when you need to stop your tongue from gossiping, and there will be times when you must stop it from responding to gossip. Valerius Maximus related a story showing this truth:

> Xenocrates... was there when some men were gossiping maliciously, but he kept completely silent. One of them asked him why he alone was holding his tongue, and he said, "Because I have often regretted saying something, but I have never regretted keeping silent."[25]

Holding your tongue and keeping silent is never wrong, unless you are silent about your faith because of fear. If you become a leader in the world or in the church, you will be faced with the sharp slanderous tongues of those who oppose you. What do you do when you are the victim of slander? Consider the approach of Mark Twain:

> Besides, I had learned, a good while before that, that it is not wise to keep the fire going under a slander unless you can get some large advantage out of keeping it alive. Few slanders can stand the wear of silence.[26]

The tongue has unbelievable power. With your words, you may cause others deep pain they will carry the rest of their lives. And, if you are not careful, careless words that slip off your tongue at the wrong moment can become a self-inflicted wound that will cause you to experience great pain. Valerius Maximus shared a story that shows the harm we can do to ourselves when we have a loose tongue:

> I shall add the story of two men who were acquitted through the fault of their accusers. Marcus Flavius was brought on trial before the people by Gaius Valerius, an aedile. When he had been found guilty by the votes of fourteen of the tribes, he shouted out that an innocent man was being ruined. Valerius replied in an equally loud voice that he did not care whether he was being ruined as an innocent man or a guilty one as long as he was being ruined. The violence of this remark presented his opponent with the votes of

---

25. Maximus, *Memorable Deeds and Sayings*, 241.
26. Twain, *Autobiography*, Loc. 4617–19.

all the remaining tribes. Valerius had crushed his enemy into the ground, but when he was confident that his enemy was definitely finished, he raised him up again and lost his victory at the very moment of winning it.[27]

If you are not careful in what you say, your words could lead to your own destruction. Talking behind the back of others, lying, cursing—those are not the only sins of the tongue. Our tongue gets in trouble when we say one thing, but do not make good on it, or when we are loose with our tongue and say too much to the wrong person. In this way, the tongue can be personally destructive when our words come back to haunt us.

Alexander Hamilton and Thomas Jefferson were very different men. They worked together in George Washington's cabinet where they were friends and often spent time talking together. Actually, Hamilton did most of the talking. Jefferson was a proper gentleman, never willing to engage in public or private disputes. Unlike Hamilton, who loved to debate, Jefferson hated controversy and was careful in revealing his true thoughts.

Jefferson was a master of saying what a person wanted to hear, while keeping his own views to himself. John Adams called Jefferson "Shadow Man." Hamilton was the opposite; he could not control his tongue. "For Hamilton, unable to govern his tongue or his pen, his habit of self-exposure eventually placed him at the mercy of the tightly controlled Jefferson."[28] Because of his loose tongue, Hamilton was eventually destroyed politically and Jefferson, who carefully guarded his words, became the president of the United States.

Similarly, James warned us to watch our tongues because an uncontrolled tongue can be personally destructive. This is the power of the tongue. With it, you can bless God and you can also cause much harm to yourself and to others. We need to guard against an uncontrolled tongue.

We also must avoid speaking rashly. We all know that rash speaking is a very negative characteristic in people. Those who speak without thinking speak rashly, without having carefully weighed the effect of their words. Sometimes we do not speak when we need to speak. Other times we speak when we should have just listened.

During the Second World War and the preparation for D-Day, officers far below General Eisenhower were tempted to make speeches to inspire the troops. On one particular boat heading across the English Channel

---

27. Maximus, *Memorable Deeds and Sayings*, 268.
28. Chernow, *Alexander Hamilton*, 320.

with six hundred British soldiers who were about to storm Gold Beach, U.S. Navy Lt. Tony Duke thought he would give a speech over the ship's loudspeaker. Thoughts of Shakespeare and Henry V ran through his mind. He recounted that just before he made his speech a British army colonel came up to the bridge:

> [He] put his hand on my shoulder, I'll never forget it, and said, "Careful, young fellow. Most of my men have seen the worst of desert warfare and a good many of them were in France and evacuated through Dunkirk. So I'd advise you to go easy, go quick, and don't get dramatic or emotional." My own emotions were thumping, straining inside of me, but I took his lead and made a very simple announcement. I realized later that I would have made a real jackass out of myself if I'd let go with exactly how I did feel.[29]

We should always take great care to make sure we have weighed our words in any situation. How much more should we weigh our words when we are standing in the presence of our God at church on the Lord's Day? If, for example, you and I were privileged to bring our needs and requests to the White House or to Buckingham Palace, we would prepare our words carefully, would be on our best behavior, and would wear our best clothes. How much more important it is when we come to the throne of Almighty God in prayer and worship.

FLATTERY

Flattery is another sin of the tongue. Flattery occurs when a person says something behind the back of another that they will not say to their face. A very common form of flattery occurs in the workplace when a subordinate seeking advancement will say to their superior what they think they want to hear.

A major problem with flattery is that it causes one to be placed in a situation that they do not really want. Consider the wisdom of the philosopher Diogenes, who was at Syracuse rinsing vegetables, when Aristippus, a member of the king's court, said to him:

> "If you would agree to flatter Dionysius (a tyrant king), you wouldn't have to eat those." And Diogenes answered, "You've got

---

29. Ambrose, *D-Day*, 171–72.

it wrong. If you would agree to eat them, you wouldn't have to flatter Dionysius."[30]

At its core, flattery is thinly-disguised lying. Aristippus lied about his support and love for Dionysius so that he could get what he wanted from him.

Flattery is the weapon of choice for false teachers. In Romans 16:18, the apostle Paul says that false teachers use smooth words and flattery to deceive the hearts of the naïve. Paul says that such liars are not serving God, but their own belly.

HYPOCRISY

> If we say we have fellowship with Him, and walk in darkness, we lie and do not practice the truth.
> (1 John 1:6)

According to the apostle John, if we say we are followers of Christ and yet our lifestyle is just like the world, our claim to be a Christian is a lie. Why is that the case? Because we are not practicing the truth. Fellowship with Christ means that we are practicing truth and living according to the Bible. This means that we do not do the things God's word says are sin. We might fall short, we still sin, but we do not continually practice sin.

It is hypocrisy to act one way in public and another in private. It is playing the role of the hypocrite when a person condemns the actions of others, and their own actions are just as bad or even worse. Polybius says:

> It is very easy to find fault with others, and one notices as a rule that those who are readiest to blame others err most in the conduct of their own life.[31]

In Matthew 23, Jesus repeated the phrase "Woe unto you" to the Pharisees. "Woe to you, hypocrites," and he listed out numerous aspects of their hypocrisy. Jesus knew the hardness of their hearts. They were like whitewashed tombs, clean and beautiful on the outside, but on the inside nothing but dead men's bones. "Woe unto you, scribes and Pharisees, hypocrites!" These awful words are repeated like a chant of condemnation and warning. Nothing is more hated by God than hypocrisy.

---

30. Maximus, *Memorable Deeds and Sayings*, 137.
31. Polybius, *Histories*, Loc. 10577-78.

Seeking Virtue

God does not hate the hypocrite, but the hypocrisy in their hearts. It was hypocrisy that was keeping these men from a true relationship with God. They were religious playactors, living a lie. On the outside, they had the appearance of holiness: they were praying; they read their Scriptures; they pretended to worship God. However, they did not possess real faith. They were quick to point out the errors of men around them, but they were more guilty than them all because in their hearts they had no true faith or love for God. Instead, they loved the praise of man. Also, we must understand that hypocrisy will eventually be exposed.

Plutarch told the story of a Messenian named Dinocrates who had travelled to Rome to beg Emperor Titus to send an army to deliver his city from the Achaeans. The city of Dinocrates had been besieged and the people were on the brink of starvation.

Dinocrates was on a mission to Rome to save his people from certain death. The night before he was to meet with Titus, Dinocrates went out partying in the bars of ancient Rome. At one point in the evening, he was so drunk that he was dancing dressed in women's clothes. The next day he went before Titus, and Dinocrates had a very depressed look on his face and was urgently begging Titus to help save his people before it was too late. Titus replied:

> This will be matter for consideration; my only surprise is that a man with such purposes on his hands should be able to dance and sing at drinking parties.[32]

The actions of Dinocrates the night before exposed him as a hypocrite in the eyes of the emperor. Similarly, we can be sure that our hypocrisy will ultimately be exposed; therefore, this is a thing to avoid.

DRUNKENNESS

> And do not be *drunk* with wine, in which is dissipation; but be filled with the Spirit.
> (Eph 5:18)

In 1 Kings 16, the story is told of Elah, a young prince in the royal house of Israel. Elah had grown up a prince, the son of a hard-hearted disobedient king. When it was his turn to step into leadership, he did not have a heart that God could bless and did not possess the leadership skills of his father.

---

32. Plutarch, *Lives*, 2:513.

Elah was a man who was sold out to the party life and it was in his sin that the judgment came. On one occasion, his army was in the field, but Elah was in his steward's house partying and getting drunk.

In the text, the suddenness of God's judgment stands out. Elah was drunk in his steward's house, and the Bible says that his servant Zimri struck and killed him. The sin of Elah was the sin of drunkenness. He should have been in the field with his troops; instead he was drinking with his steward.

In the modern church culture, it is not popular to speak out against social drinking. But what does the word of God say on this subject? Throughout Scripture drunkenness is associated with God's holy judgment. For example, Jeremiah 51:7 says, "Babylon was a golden cup in the Lord's hand, that made all the earth drunk. The nations drank her wine; therefore the nations are deranged." Also, Habbakuk 2:15–16 states, "Woe to him who gives drink to his neighbor, pressing him to your bottle, even to make him drunk . . . you also, drink! And be exposed as uncircumcised. The cup of the Lord's right hand will be turned against you." Furthermore, Proverbs 23:20–21 says, "Do not mix with winebibbers or the gluttonous eaters of meat; for the drunkard and glutton will come to poverty."

People who drink and get defensive about it always say, "Why doesn't the minister preach against gluttony?" This is a valid point and God has an answer in Proverbs 23:21, where the overeater and the drinker are condemned together. Paul said in Ephesians 5:18, "Do not be drunk with wine." In Luke 12:45, Jesus said that a wicked man is one who disregards the promised coming of the Lord and he eats and drinks and gets drunk. "The master of the servant will come at a day when he is not looking for him."

This was the fate of Elah. Elah was drinking and partying, and the last thing he was expecting was to stand before God at that moment. But Zimri, the servant of the king, went in and struck him. Elah left this world and in a moment, he was in the presence of God for judgment. Diogenes records how the great philosopher Anacharsis sums up the path of drunkenness:

> It was a saying of his that the vine bore three kinds of grapes: the first of pleasure, the next of intoxication, and the third of disgust.[33]

Make no mistake, strong drink has been the ruin of many people. Getting drunk leads them to commit sins that if sober they would have never dreamed of committing. The following story demonstrates the powerful effect of alcohol and the regret felt by one who acts out under its influence.

---

33. Diogenes, *Lives of Eminent Philosophers*, 107.

Seeking Virtue

Alexander the Great had conquered most of the known world and many outside influences were now in his court. Among these influences were flatterers who sought to get themselves into favor with the victorious king.

Alexander was known for his strong work ethic and his aversion to drinking strong wine. However, for a brief time in his life he allowed himself to be influenced by the barbarian drinking habits. On one such occasion, Alexander was at a drinking party with his closest friends, as well as some of his new friends from among the barbarians who had a bad influence on him. His closest friend and advisor, Kleitos, was at the party and drinking as well. Kleitos had been harboring resentment against the barbarians, whom he felt were flattering Alexander and leading him down a self-destructive path. Some of these flatterers were praising Alexander with false praise, saying his exploits were greater than all the Greek heroes of the past, even Heracles.

Kleitos, also heavily influenced by the wine, had heard enough and said he would not allow them to disrespect the ancient heroes. He said that these flatterers were making Alexander's exploits greater than they really were and that Alexander did not achieve all of his conquests by himself.

Hearing the words of Kleitos, Alexander was offended by his friend and both, being under the influence of alcohol, escalated the tension quickly. The flatterers among the company did not let up. They increased their praise, saying that Phillip's achievements were nothing compared to Alexander's. Phillip was the father of Alexander and was greatly admired. Kleitos could no longer contain himself. He responded in anger and said that the deeds of Alexander were not as great as Phillip's. Also, he reminded Alexander that he had saved his life in a battle against the Persians. Finally, extending his right hand haughtily, he said, "This was the hand, Alexander, that saved you then." Consider the end of this tragic story as related by Arrian:

> Alexander could no longer bear Kleitos' drunken insolence. He leaped up in a fury and was restrained by his fellow banqueters. Kleitos would not stop taunting him. . . . Alexander's companions were no longer able to restrain him. He leaped up; some say that it was a spear he snatched from one of his bodyguards and used to strike Kleitos, killing him, while others say he used a sarisa snatched from one of the guards. For my part, I utterly deplore the insolence Kleitos displayed toward his king, and I pity Alexander for his misfortune: he showed himself mastered on that occasion by two vices, namely anger and drunkenness, neither of which should get the better of a sensible man. But I commend Alexander's

conduct in the aftermath, for he recognized immediately that he had committed a savage act. There are some who report that he leaned the sarisa against the wall, intending to fall on it, on the grounds that now that he had killed his friend while drunk it was dishonorable for him to live. But most historians offer a different account and say that Alexander took to his bed and lay prostrate in grief, calling out Kleitos' name and that of Kleitos' sister Lanike, who had nursed him, saying that he had after all made her a fine return for her nursing now that he was grown; for she had seen two of her own sons die fighting for him, and now he had himself killed her brother with his own hand. Again and again he called himself the murderer of his own friends, and went without food and drink for three days and completely neglected all other care of his person.[34]

This tragic story is the sad result of drunkenness. Had Alexander and Kleitos not been under the influence of alcohol, the entire situation might have been avoided. The two men loved each other and fought battles together. But drunkenness so clouded their judgment in a fit of emotional anger that one murdered the other.

Avoid strong drink, do not be filled with wine, but rather be filled with the Spirit of God.

MIXED UP PRIORITIES

> For what will it profit a man if he gains the whole world, and loses his own soul?
> (Mark 8:36)

Mixing up priorities at work or in the home frequently leads to devastating effects. Those who are wise will take the time to reflect on their priorities to assure that they are arranged in a way to give them the best opportunity for success. As important as it is to have our work and home responsibilities prioritized correctly, it is our spiritual life that requires the most diligent attention. If our spiritual life is not correctly prioritized, it will matter little how diligent we are in the other areas of our lives.

Take the example of Israel in the years following the Babylonian captivity. As a result of the policies of the Persian King Cyrus, many Jews

---

34. Arrian, *Campaigns of Alexander*, 162–64.

returned to the land and shortly thereafter, some progress was made on rebuilding the temple in Jerusalem.

After the initial efforts under Cyrus to rebuild the temple following the return to Judah of the first exiles, progress had ground to a halt. As Ezra 4:24 recorded, "Thus the work of the house of God which is at Jerusalem ceased, and it was discontinued until the second year of the reign of Darius king of Persia."

The reason the work came to a halt was due to the opposition the people of Israel were receiving from local authorities. The people who occupied the land after Israel went into captivity were not happy to see them return and did not want them to rebuild the temple. After Cyrus died, they threatened the people doing the work and registered official complaints to the Persian authorities. Cyrus's successor, Darius, studied the issue and sent back word for them to proceed rebuilding the temple. In addition, he released all of the temple supplies, including the gold and silver utensils used in the temple worship that had been taken to Babylon by Nebuchadnezzar. The Jews had the all clear, but then something happened in Jerusalem to the people: they did nothing.

They had started the work faithfully, but after the controversy and the waiting, they had no heart to resume the work to complete the temple. They were busy with their own lives, building and beautifying their own homes. They were struggling to provide for their own families, and the economy was not good. As a result, no one had the motivation in their hearts to do what needed to be done to rebuild the temple of God.

For this reason, God sent Haggai the prophet. In Haggai 1:4, God called them out for this: the people said it was not the time to build the Lord's house, but the Lord said, "Is it time for you yourselves to dwell in your paneled houses, and this temple to lie in ruins?"

Understand that the temple at this time was where God himself dwelt among the people. It was not like it is today, where the bodies of God's people are his temples. God's Spirit dwelt in the temple in Jerusalem. The people forgot that neglecting the house of God would bring ruin on their families because God's presence would not be among them.

We do the same thing today when we get our priorities mixed up. We neglect our spiritual duties, and we forget that doing so will have an effect on our lives and our families. We need to take care of the house of God first. Your body is the temple of the Holy Spirit, and your priority should be to keep your body clean from sin. Some of us need to rebuild our spiritual temples because they have been neglected far too long. What good will it do for you to have a beautiful home or a great job but have the temple of the Holy Spirit, which is your body, laid waste in sin and clutter? Paul said in Philippians 2:21, "For all seek their own, not the things which are of Christ Jesus." Mixing up priorities can have a devastating effect on you and your family.

Salmon Chase was secretary of the treasury under President Abraham Lincoln and later chief justice of the Supreme Court. His first wife was named Kitty. She was an attractive young woman whom he loved greatly. Sadly, Kitty died in childbirth eighteen months after they were married.

Chase was so grieved he could barely function. His grief was compounded by guilt, for he was away on business in Philadelphia when Kitty died, having been assured by her doctor that she would recover. "Oh how I accused myself of folly and wickedness in leaving her when yet sick," he confided in his diary. "How I mourned that the prospect of a little addition to my reputation . . . should have tempted me away."

For months afterward, Chase berated himself; he was a Christian and feared that Kitty had died without affirming her faith. He felt he had not pushed her firmly enough toward God. "Oh if I had not contented myself with a few conversations on the subject of religion," he lamented in his diary, "if I had tried harder to persuade her . . . she might have been before her death enrolled among the professed followers of the Lamb. But I procrastinated and now she is gone."[35]

Chase had mixed-up priorities and it cost him dearly. We need to learn from the mistakes of those who come before us. We need to prioritize our relationship with the Lord and his word. Do not put work or even the needs of your own family ahead of your commitment to following the Lord. If you will seek the Lord first, he has promised to give you everything else you need.

---

35. Goodwin, *Team of Rivals*, 42.

Chapter 5

Things You Need

And my God shall supply all your need *according to His riches in glory by Christ Jesus.*

(PHILIPPIANS 4:19)

Do not doubt that God can supply anything you need. In 2 Kings 4, the story is told of a widow who came to Elisha the prophet. She was a believer in the one true God. The woman was in debt, and the creditor was coming to take her two sons and sell them into slavery as payment for the debt.

The woman came to Elisha begging for help. Elisha asked her if she had anything of value in the house. The only thing she possessed was a bowl of oil. Elisha said to the woman in 2 Kings 4:3–4, "Go, borrow vessels from everywhere, from all your neighbors—empty vessels; do not gather just a few. And when you have come in, you shall shut the door behind you and your sons; then pour it into all those vessels, and set aside the full ones."

The widow did as instructed and took all of the vessels she could borrow from her neighbors, put them in the house, closed the door, took the little bowl of oil and filled them up until every vessel that she had collected was filled to the top. Then the oil stopped coming. Elisha then said to her, "Sell the oil, pay your debt and live on the rest."

This is much like what God invites us to do: take all of your needs, all of those "empty vessels," and place them before the Lord. Ask God to fill them up and answer every need. Some of our needs are physical. We need food to eat, clothing to wear, and shelter. We need a job; we need money to pay bills. Ask God to meet every temporal need you have.

Perhaps you are a blessed one, and all your physical needs are met and you have plenty of money. But what about your spiritual needs? Remember that "to whom much is given, much is expected." You also need spiritual help to grow in your faith and minister to others. In our work, we need wisdom and courage. In days of trial and pain, we need patience. We have personal needs, family needs, spiritual needs, and bodily needs.

If you do not have any needs, it may be because you are not even trying to live in faith. Our need is an occasion for the blessing of God. That is what gives God the opportunity to help us and bless us: we have a need. If I do not have the need, God cannot help me, nor can he bless me, nor can he fill me. If I am full already; if I am all-sufficient; if I say, "I am rich and have need of nothing," what can God do for me?

If I am empty; if I am poor; if I am in need; if I am distressed; if I am disappointed; if I am in despair; if I am dejected; then I have an opportunity to receive from God a precious and wonderful blessing. My need is the occasion of the blessing of God. The apostle Paul says, "My God will supply all your needs." He will fill up those empty vessels. But you must bring them to God.

In this chapter the topic is the "things we need" to live a virtuous life. We know that God has promised to provide for our physical needs, but we tend to forget that God has promised to supply *all of our needs*. As will be seen there are many other things that we need besides money if we desire to grow in virtue.

BOLDNESS

> The wicked flee when no one pursues, but the righteous are *bold* as a lion.
> (Prov 28:1)

As believers in the resurrected Christ, who are filled with the Holy Spirit of God, we should be bold in our faith. When one considers the incredible promises God has given to us—to be with us in all circumstances, to watch over us and care for us—there is nothing that should cause us to fear.

If you are living in fear, you need to ask yourself why. Solomon said, "The wicked flee when no one pursues." If a Christian has sin in their life, it is a cause of fear. The presence of sin often produces paranoia in the life of a believer. They will run when no one is really pursuing them. They know that the sin in their life has placed them outside of God's favor. To be bold requires that we not only believe in the Lord, but that we walk with him. We must confess our sin and walk boldly in faith.

To be bold requires that we speak and act truthfully in every circumstance of life. For a Christian to be bold requires the willingness to offend if necessary. Christians do not want to offend because of a disagreeable personality, or by speaking at an inappropriate time. But we are required to speak the truth.

Sometimes, speaking the truth about salvation to a friend who does not yet believe may strain the friendship. That is a risk we must be willing to take. If we truly believe what we say we believe about life and death, we have no choice but to be bold and warn those we love, even if it is offensive to their ears.

Someone once said, "There are times when the harp must be exchanged for the trumpet." People do not get mad if you play a harp next to them. Actually, they might appreciate it. But if you blow a trumpet in their ear they generally have a different response. The Christian must have courage to sound the warning. If someone you love is doing something that is going to lead to their death apart from Christ, you do not play a harp. You blow a trumpet!

As you live your life and live out your faith, you need to acquire boldness. It takes boldness to share your faith to friends, who might reject you. It takes boldness to live your faith at work when it might cost you a promotion. But in the light of church history and the death of the martyrs of the faith, such a sacrifice pales in comparison.

At the beginning of the Baptist church movement, Thomas Helwys wrote a book entitled *The Mystery of Iniquity*. Helwys lived in England during a time when church and state were united and it was illegal to separate from the state church. In his book, Helwys argued that there should be complete religious freedom for all people to worship as they please. After the book was published, Helwys boldly sent a copy to King James of England, with a message written on the inside just to the king:

> Heare, o king, and dispise not ye counsel of ye poore, and let their complaints come before thee. The king is a mortal man, and not God

THINGS YOU NEED

> therefore hath no power over ye immortal soules of his subjects, to make lawes and ordinances for them, and to set spirtuall Lords over them.
>
> If the king have authority to make spirtuall Lords and lawes, then he is an immortall God, and not a mortall man.
> O king, be not seduced by deceivers to sin so against God whome thou oughtest to obey, nor against thy poore subjects who ought and will obey thee in all things with body life and goods, or els let their lives be taken from ye earth.
> God save ye king.
> Spittlefield neare London.
>
> Tho: Helwys[1]

This is a bold statement to make to a king who has the power of life and death over you. Not long after Helwys sent this to the king, he was arrested and eventually died in prison.

Boldness is a thing you need. The Christian life is not one that is to be lived in the shadows of society. We are called to be lights in the world, showing the way to salvation. No one lights a candle and then hides it under a basket. We are saved and called to shine our lights brightly in a dark world. It takes boldness to live in the light.

WISDOM

> *Wisdom* is the principal thing; therefore get *wisdom*. And in all your getting, get understanding.
> (Prov 4:7)

According to Solomon, wisdom goes to the person who most diligently looks for it. The spoils go to the one who is the most committed, the one who wants it the most and who is willing to sacrifice to get it. The wisdom that God gives is more valuable than the gold and silver of this world.

In the days of the California Gold Rush, those who found the gold were the ones who were the most prolific in moving dirt. Death Valley, California, got its name from the fact that so many died there looking for treasure.

When Mark Twain was a young man, he moved to California and took part in the rush for gold. He described the scene in California as

---

1. Estep, *The Anabaptist Story*, 293.

Seeking Virtue

thousands of prospectors were sinking shafts into the mountains, hoping to find riches. There were so many people working in the mines that the population underground was as much as above ground.

Twain arrived with little experience but, like everyone else, he thought that he was going to strike it rich in no time. On one occasion, he was working in his mine, but the more experienced partners in this mine had retired for the day. The partners had been skeptical of the mine and felt it was going to be what they called a "wildcat" mine that produced no gold. They even ridiculed Twain for his youthful optimism.

While Twain was walking around the mine, something caught his eye. It looked like gold and he quickly uncovered a large gold-colored rock. He picked up his golden rock and in his mind, he was imagining the riches he had just unearthed. Even more joyous however, was the thought of the reaction of his partners. Twain quickly made his way to the campsite, rehearsing in his mind how he was going to unveil his riches to his doubting partners. Twain said to his partners:

> "Gentlemen," said I, "I don't say anything—*I* haven't been around, you know, and of course don't know anything—but all I ask of you is to cast your eye on *that*, for instance, and tell me what you think of it!" and I tossed my treasure before them. There was an eager scramble for it, and a closing of heads together over it under the candle-light. Then old Ballou said: "Think of it? I think it is nothing but a lot of granite rubbish and nasty glittering mica that isn't worth ten cents an acre!"
>
> So vanished my dream. So melted my wealth away. So toppled my airy castle to the earth and left me stricken and forlorn.
>
> Moralizing, I observed, then, that "all that glitters is not gold."[2]

It is much the same in our search for wisdom: "All that glitters is not gold." God's wisdom is more valuable than gold, but it is found in only one place. Any other so-called wisdom that does not come from the true source is nothing but worthless mica dug out of a wildcat mine. The wisdom that God offers us is not scarce. In fact, there is wisdom available in abundance. You just need to know where to look for it and then be diligent to seek for it like you would great treasure. As Proverbs 2:4–6 says, "If you seek her as silver and search for her as for hidden treasures, then you will understand the fear of the Lord, and find the knowledge of God. For the Lord gives wisdom."

---

2. Twain, *Innocents Abroad*, 680.

God has wisdom stored up in his treasuries. It is there for the taking, or for the asking. But it only goes to the diligent, the spiritually hungry, those who are prolific in their search.

The problem with most people is that they are looking for wisdom in the things of this world. They seek to attain worldly wisdom for the purpose of worldly gain. The treasures most people want are material. They spend their lives chasing and digging for the treasures of this world: silver and gold and worldly glory. Only in the end do they discover they were searching for the wrong kind of treasure. The Roman statesman Seneca gave the following suggestions on acquiring wisdom:

> But how does one acquire wisdom? By practicing it daily, in however modest a degree; by examining your conduct of each day at its close; by being harsh to your own faults and lenient to those of others; by associating with those who excel you in wisdom and virtue; by taking some acknowledged sage as your invisible counselor and judge. You will be helped by reading the philosophers; not outline stories of philosophy, but the original works; "give over hoping that you can skim, by means of epitomes, the wisdom of distinguished men." "Every one of these men will send you away happier and more devoted, no one of them will allow you to depart empty-handed. . . . What happiness, and what a noble old age, await him who has given himself into their personage!" Read good books many times, rather than many books; travel slowly, and not too much; "the spirit cannot mature into unity unless it has checked its curiosity and its wanderings." "The primary sign of a well-ordered mind is a man's ability to remain in one place and linger in his own company." Avoid crowds. "Men are more wicked together than separately. If you are forced to be in a crowd, then most of all you should withdraw into yourself."[3]

A prime characteristic of biblical wisdom is prudence. According to the dictionary, to be prudent means "to be shrewd in the management of practical affairs; to be cautious, discreet . . . judicious, foresighted, sensible."[4]

In Proverbs 1:4, Solomon wrote that God inspired him to write the Proverbs in order to give prudence to the simple and "to the young man knowledge and discretion." In other words, to make us shrewd in this world.

The idea of shrewdness often has a negative connotation. We call people shrewd who are often crafty in an evil sense or who take advantage

---

3. Durant, *Caesar and Christ*, 305.
4. *Merriam-Webster's Dictionary*, 650.

Seeking Virtue

of others. However, the biblical idea of shrewdness or prudence describes someone who considers life with eyes wide open; a person who can size up a situation and knows what is going on around them. A person with prudence is one who is discerning, who looks at a circumstance and sees all the possibilities and opportunities and makes sensible decisions using the word of God as his or her guide. The wisdom that God gives dwells with the prudent, one who is shrewd in decision-making. Wisdom does not attach itself to a person who is rash, driven by emotions, selfish, and insecure.

Insecurity is an issue for many of us and unless we find our inner peace through the Holy Spirit and the word of God, we will fail to find wisdom and end up playing the fool. Proverbs 22:3 says, "A prudent man foresees evil and hides himself; but the simple pass on and are punished." Insecurity will cause a person to "pass on," in other words, to make rash decisions without thinking ahead. What follows is punishment.

How many marriage disasters would be avoided if people would use the prudence that God's word provides? How many financial disasters would be avoided if people would use prudence—if they would be shrewd with their money, not live beyond their means, and be faithful in their giving? But most people, driven by fear and insecurity, make foolish decisions not based on God's word. They bypass wisdom and the result is punishment, not only from God, but also from the natural consequences of their poor choices. If you desire biblical wisdom, then start living with prudence and make decisions informed by God's word.

Solomon wrote in Proverbs 3:21–26, "My son . . . keep sound wisdom and discretion. So they will be life to your soul and grace to your neck. Then you will walk safely in your way and your foot will not stumble. . . . Do not be afraid of sudden terror, nor of trouble from the wicked when it comes, for the Lord will be your confidence, and will keep your foot from being caught."

Wisdom is something that God possesses, and he gives to those who will ask for it. It is then our responsibility to keep it and to bind it around our necks. When we have that wisdom, we experience true confidence for living. Whether we are in the day of prosperity or in the day of adversity, because wisdom is ours to possess, we are reminded to do what Solomon has told us to do in Ecclesiastes 7:13, "Consider the work of God; For who can make straight what He has made crooked?"

Wisdom teaches us to look upon our present circumstances and consider them as the product of God's will. We cannot control the circumstances of our lives. Therefore, it is our calling to accept our situation as a duty. Solomon says if you are in a day of prosperity, rejoice and be thankful for it. But the wise will read the word, and notice it is but a day, only a day, and that another kind of day will follow. If God uses all of life's circumstances for our good, the wise will reflect upon this promise. We cannot discover God's purpose in allowing affliction unless we consider and reflect.

According to Solomon, God is in control of our lives. For some of us, he has made our way straight. But for others he has made their way crooked with adversity. Who can straighten what God has made crooked? The answer is no one. God's providential care is where we need to place our trust. Wisdom teaches us to have faith in God. We do not know what is ahead of us. God has designed the world in this way.

Worldly people want to know their future, so they turn to the psychics or the horoscopes. These things do not belong in the life of a Christian. Such things are an insult to God. God has kept the times and seasons in his own hand. He mingles crooked and straight things in man's experience. As a result, we are not able to guess with certainty what is coming. We are thus compelled to lead a life of faith.

When we live with wisdom, we do not need to know the future. We simply rejoice in the good times, and in the bad times we reflect. We learn from these, like David wrote in Psalm 119:67, "Before I was afflicted I went astray, but now I keep your word." The truth is that the times of affliction drive us back to God. If God makes something crooked, he is able to make it straight. Perhaps he will ask us to work with him to get the job done. But, if he wants it to stay crooked, we must not argue with him.

We do not fully understand all the works of God, but we do know that "he has made everything beautiful in its time" (Eccl 3:11). This includes the things we may think are twisted and ugly. Adversity breeds greatness into us, and God uses the crooked path to teach us to trust him. Do not curse adversity in your life, but seek wisdom. She will teach you to have confidence in the providential care of God.

The Bible is very clear that wisdom is a commodity that we should seek and that true, life-giving wisdom only comes from God. However, there is wisdom in this world that we can gain and use to make us better people.

In the ancient world of the Greeks and Romans, philosophers were held in high regard. Schools developed around successful philosophers, and there were competing schools. It was a sign of social status to be associated with the greatest philosophers. The most famous philosophers in the ancient world are referred to as the "Seven Sages." Each of these men were set apart from all others and recognized by their contemporaries as the wisest among men. Valerius Maximus gave us a summary of the story of the Seven Sages:

> The mention of this man reminds me that I should talk about the moderation of the Seven Sages. In the region of Miletus some fishermen were drawing a net and a certain man bought their catch. A very heavy tripod made of gold was pulled out of the net, and an argument arose, with the fishermen claiming that they had sold only the fish they had caught and the buyer saying that he had bought whatever they were lucky enough to catch. Because it was such an unusual occurrence and because such a large sum of money was involved, the decision was referred to the entire people of that state. The people decided that they should consult Apollo at Delphi to find out which of the men should be awarded the table. The god replied that it should be given to the man who surpassed the others in wisdom, and these were his words:
> "Who is the first of all in wisdom? I declare that the tripod is his."
> So the people of Miletus agreed that they should give the table to Thales. He handed it over to Bias, Bias handed it over to Pittacus, Pittacus gave it to another man, and so on through the entire circle of the Seven Sages, until it finally came to Solon; and Solon handed over the honor and prize for the greatest wisdom to Apollo himself.[5]

The Seven Sages were the most famous and wisest men of their age. Kings paid them respect and all wanted to hear their wisdom. What follows are the "apothegms" of these sages. An apothegm is a wise saying, similar to a proverb. We might refer to it as a maxim to live by. They are all well worth pondering:

Apothegm of Thales:

> Of all things that are, the most ancient is God, for he is uncreated.
> The most beautiful is the universe, for it is God's workmanship.
> The greatest is space, for it holds all things.
> The swiftest is mind, for it speeds everywhere.
> The strongest, necessity, for it masters all.

---

5. Maximus, *Memorable Deeds and Sayings*, 128.

The wisest, time, for it brings everything to light.[6]

Proverb of Thales:

Know thyself.[7]

Apothegm of Solon:

Nothing too much.[8]

Apothegm of Pittacus:

Know thine opportunity.[9]

Apothegm of Bias:

Most men are bad.[10]

Apothegm of Cleobulus:

Moderation is best.[11]

---

6. Diogenes, *Lives of Eminent Philosophers*, 37.
7. Diogenes, *Lives of Eminent Philosophers*, 41.
8. Diogenes, *Lives of Eminent Philosophers*, 65.
9. Diogenes, *Lives of Eminent Philosophers*, 81.
10. Diogenes, *Lives of Eminent Philosophers*, 91.
11. Diogenes, *Lives of Eminent Philosophers*, 97.

Apothegm of Periander:

Practice makes perfect.[12]

Wisdom by Thales

Being asked what is difficult, he replied, "To know oneself." "What is easy?" "To give advice to another." "What is most pleasant?" "Success." "What is the divine?" "That which has neither beginning nor end."[13]

Chilon on What is Hard:

What is hard? "To keep a secret, to employ leisure well, to be able to bear an injury."[14]

Solon's Counsel to Men:

Put more trust in nobility of character than in an oath. Never tell a lie. Pursue worthy aims. Do not be rash to make friends and, when once they are made, do not drop them. Learn to obey before you command. In giving advice seek to help, not to please, your friend. Be led by reason. Shun evil company. Honour the gods, reverence parents.[15]

Some of the most common wisdom sayings even today have their origin in the ancient philosophers. As Christians, we can receive wisdom from any source, even pagan philosophers. However, we must never neglect searching for the godly wisdom that is only found in his word.

---

12. Diogenes, *Lives of Eminent Philosophers*, 103.
13. Diogenes, *Lives of Eminent Philosophers*, 37.
14. Diogenes, *Lives of Eminent Philosophers*, 71.
15. Diogenes, *Lives of Eminent Philosophers*, 61.

DISCERNMENT

> Beloved, do not believe every spirit, but test the spirits, whether they are of God; because many false prophets have gone out into the world.
> (1 John 4:1)

Discernment is different from wisdom. Wisdom is a gift from God, available to all who seek after it. Discernment is an act of the will. A person is called "discerning" when he or she acts or makes a good choice based on personal study and reason. As Christians, we are to "test the spirits" before following the advice of anyone. You need discernment; it acts as a guard over your life. The Roman historian Tacitus related the following story that gives a vivid picture of what discernment looks like:

> When seeking occult guidance Tiberius would retire to the top of his house, with a single tough, illiterate former slave as confidant. Those astrologers whose skill Tiberius had decided to test were escorted to him by this man over pathless, precipitous ground; for the house overhung a cliff. Then, on their way down, if they were suspected of unreliability or fraudulence, the ex-slave hurled them into the sea below, so that no betrayer of the secret proceedings should survive. Thrasyllus, after reaching Tiberius by this steep route, had impressed him, when interrogated, by his intelligent forecasts of future events-including Tiberius' accession. Tiberius then inquired if Thrasyllus had cast his own horoscope. How did it appear for the current year and day? Thrasyllus, after measuring the positions and distances of the stars, hesitated, then showed alarm. The more he looked, the greater became his astonishment and fright. Then he cried that a critical and perhaps fatal emergency was upon him. Tiberius clasped him, commending his divination of peril and promising he would escape it. Thrasyllus was admitted among his closest friends; his pronouncements were regarded as oracular.[16]

This is an extreme example, but Tiberius had an almost fool proof way to "test the spirits." We need to be just as diligent and discerning in testing what we see and hear. Living without discernment opens a Christian up to being deceived and following lies. We must use discernment because false teachers are real. They occupy pulpits, preaching in the name of Jesus, but they secretly bring in destructive heresies.

---

16. Tacitus, *Annals of Imperial Rome*, 210.

A heresy is any teaching that changes or dilutes or misinterprets God's holy word. It does not matter how big a preacher's church is; we still must use discernment. Jesus warned in Matthew 24:24–25, "For false christs and false prophets will rise and show great signs and wonders to deceive, if possible, even the elect. See, I have told you beforehand."

In other words, you are without excuse if you allow yourself to be deceived. Jesus tests us with false teachers to see if we will love him more than the world. People who fall victim to false teachers are guilty of not using discernment in regard to what they hear.

Often, those who follow false teaching do it for worldly reasons. For some, it is the promise that false teachers give regarding money. They say, "God wants you to be rich." Many desire to be rich and follow their teachings. Or, the false teacher echoes the world, saying, "God loves us all the same, we are all God's children, do not judge, do not call someone else a sinner just because they view things differently than you."

False teachers take a biblical truth, such as loving everyone, and twist it subtly and make love mean something that it does not mean. It is not love to fail to warn a lost sinner or a saved sinner about the consequences of their sin. It is not love to be tolerant of behaviors that Scripture condemns. True love warns and begs for those lost in sin to turn to Christ. Paul wrote in Galatians 1:8, "But even if we, or an angel from heaven, preach any other gospel to you than what we have preached to you, let him be accursed."

How can we know if the one claiming to speak for God is lying or telling the truth? Discernment carries the connotation of judgment. We are to judge the words of man by the word of God. This is using discernment. There are too many Christians failing to use discernment. They basically believe everything they read and hear. Now, more than ever, we must use discernment in what we hear.

Discernment also prompts us to do what is right in all situations. It is the ability to assess a situation and do what is just and right. The Golden Rule is to be acted upon: "Do unto others as we would that they should do unto us." Doing justly requires that we do right things to others, that we not take advantage of others, that we not defraud others, that we not profit when those profits do not come to us in a right manner.

Valerius Maximus told the story of a Roman general named Camillus who was besieging a city named Falerii. A schoolteacher pretended to bring a large number of boys from noble families out for a walk, but led them over to the Roman camp. If the boys had been taken captive, there was no doubt the people of Falerii would surrender to the general.

As Camillus watched this man leading this group of children out from the walls and towards his camp, he was disgusted by it. He ordered that the boys be sent back. He tied up the teacher, gave each of the boys a rod, and had them beat the teacher all the way back into the city, with their parents watching from the city walls.

The people of Falerii were so moved by this act of justice that they surrendered to the general.[17] They were defeated by kindness and justice rather than by arms. The Roman general used great discernment to recognize the injustice being done by this man and refused to take advantage of the situation. He acted justly and, in the end, was rewarded for it.

Just actions are required by God, both justice towards our fellow man and to God. But there is no real justice without discernment.

INTEGRITY

> Then these men said, We shall not find any charge against this Daniel unless we find it against him concerning the law of his God. (Dan 6:5)

The men who spoke these words were colleagues of the prophet Daniel and served with him as administrators under the Persian king. However, Daniel was much loved and trusted by the king because of his integrity, which was causing the other administrators to get frustrated. They then conspired to catch Daniel in some scandal so they could accuse him before the king. After much effort, they concluded that there was nothing of which to accuse Daniel, unless it concerned his faith in God.

The Persian kings loved integrity in their governors and demanded it. Those Persian kings ruled over vast areas of the world, and their appointed administrators were vital in the effectiveness of the empire.

About a century after Daniel, the ruler of the Persians was King Cambyses. He appointed Otanes to the position of judge or administrator to replace his father. This was the same position that had been held by Daniel. The father of this Otanes was a man named Sisamnes, one of the royal judges, whom King Cambyses had punished for accepting a bribe and giving an unjust verdict. Herodotus described what happened:

---

17. Maximus, *Memorable Deeds and Sayings*, 217.

The king had ordered that his throat be cut and his entire body flayed; and after his skin was removed, strips were cut from it and stretched on the throne on which he had sat while rendering judgments. The judge whom Cambyses appointed to replace Sisamnes was actually the son of the very same Sisamnes he had executed and flayed, and Cambyses instructed this son to remember what throne he was sitting on whenever he was acting as judge.[18]

Why was Cambyses so brutal? Because the royal judges, of whom Daniel was one, were known to be corrupt, power-hungry, brutal men who stole from the coffers of the king.

Darius appointed three judges: two of them were corrupt, but not Daniel. Daniel had such integrity that his presence and his accounting were making the others look bad, perhaps even endangering them. Adding to the urgency of these wicked men was the fact that Daniel was about to be promoted to a position over them.

There seem to be certain maxims that are always true in life. One of them is this: anytime a person reaches a place of prominence, they are going to face adversity. The price of success is the envy of others. Envy is one of the ugliest things in this world; it makes people act insanely. Solomon complained in Ecclesiastes 4:4, "I saw that for all toil and every skillful work a man is envied by his neighbor." Too often, the better a man is the worse he is thought of by his rivals.

Daniel was envied because he had a more excellent spirit than his neighbors. Those who envied Daniel did not just want him fired from his job; they wanted him dead.

Solomon wrote in Proverbs 27:4, "Wrath is cruel, and anger is outrageous, but who can stand before envy?" Daniel's enemies set spies upon him, to observe him in the management of his public office. They "sought to find occasion against him," on which to ground an accusation concerning the kingdom. They were looking for some instance of neglect or partiality, or a hasty word spoken, or a person treated unjustly, or a crooked business dealing. They could not believe that the public face of Daniel was the same as the private. Surely Daniel had some secret scheme, a skeleton in the closet, a past mistake, anything that would prove Daniel was not as holy as the king thought. They looked closely, but could not find anything. Daniel was squeaky clean! They could find nothing on which to accuse him. Daniel always acted honestly and with integrity.

18. Herodotus, *Histories*, 376.

As a believer in Jesus Christ you must be aware that people are watching you. When your neighbors see you get up and go to church on Sunday, they are also watching how you live on Monday through Saturday. When your coworkers see that Bible in your car or find out you go to church and are a believer, they are going to carefully watch how you conduct business because they are looking to see if you live with integrity.

How can we possess a spirit of integrity? We hear architects and engineers say, "This building has structural integrity." That means the structure is resting upon an unseen foundation that is deep, hidden, and solid.

Jesus addressed this point in his Sermon on the Mount when he spoke about the wise builder who built his home on the foundation of solid rock. He was speaking of the person of integrity who hears the word of God and puts it into practice. Integrity is a matter of the heart. It is rooted in something that is unseen. A Christian man or woman of integrity has an unseen foundation deep within them. It is hidden and solid as a rock: the word of God provides that foundation. Daniel's excellent spirit was characterized by such integrity. We need to live with integrity if we are going to lead a virtuous life.

KNOWLEDGE

> The heart of the prudent acquires *knowledge*, and the ear of the wise seeks *knowledge*.
> (Prov 18:15)

The Scripture describes knowledge as a commodity that every person is responsible for seeking and finding. Without knowledge you are destined to be trapped in the desires of the flesh. You will know nothing except what your stomach tells you.

Knowledge of history, science, math, and above all, knowledge of your Creator will open up life to you. Seek after knowledge, desire wisdom, and in all your getting, get understanding.

Plutarch related the story of the Greek general Demetrius, who had taken over a city in which lived the famous philosopher Stilpo. Demetrius wanted to show respect to Stilpo, so he called for him, and begged to know whether anything belonging to him had been taken. "No," replied Stilpo, "I have not met with anyone to take away knowledge."[19]

When your most valuable possession is knowledge, no one can take it away from you. When someone takes anything else you possess, if you have knowledge, you will not care that it is gone.

God spoke through Hosea the prophet and said, "My people are destroyed from lack of knowledge." The knowledge that the Lord wants his children to obtain is the knowledge of his word, the knowledge of himself and how he relates to his children. The children of Israel were destroyed because of their lack of knowledge, and often the same thing happens to Christians in the present age.

FRIENDSHIP

> The soul of Jonathan was knit to the soul of David, and Jonathan loved him as his own soul.
> (1 Sam 18:1)

All Christians need faithful friends to walk with them on their journey. Cultivating Christian friendships will fortify your life on many different levels.

Jonathan was a true friend to David. On the first day they met each other, David was carrying the head of Goliath in his hand when Saul asked him, "Whose son are you, young man?" The Scripture says, "The soul of Jonathan was knit with the soul of David." The word rendered "knit" literally means "knotted," tied together firmly by unbreakable bonds.

Jonathan was a man with genuine faith. He too trusted God in battle, but not even Jonathan was willing to tangle with Goliath. Jonathan and David shared the same spirit of faith, but Jonathan saw something special in David and loved him for it. Jonathan's love for David and his friendship were the result of faith. Jonathan observed the incredible faith of David and it inspired him. This is a significant point.

How do you choose your close friends? What is the motivation for your friendship? Every person should consider the character of those with whom they are friends. Is the basis of your friendship something base and

---

19. Plutarch, *Lives*, 1:450.

sinful? Some are friends because they are drinking buddies, or fishing buddies.

Of course, there is nothing wrong with going fishing with your buddies, but what is it that has inspired you to be friends with the people with whom you are friends? Jonathan was attached to David because he was inspired by his great faith. God was the center of their friendship. When you have a friend like that, you have a friend indeed! Petty disagreements do not break up that kind of friendship.

First Samuel 18 noted that Jonathan and David made a covenant with one another. The idea of a covenant means that David and Jonathan based their friendship on mutual commitments to live for the Lord and to glorify him. It is a powerful thing in a person's life to have a friend who is committed to the Lord and committed to holding his or her friends accountable to walk with the Lord.

This is what it means to be brothers and sisters in Christ. We should have other Christians we are committed to, whom we love and admire, who will call us out if we miss church and if we are being worldly. If we have a friend who expects us to live for Christ, then we have a true friend.

This is one of the great purposes of the church. It is in the fellowship of believers where we form those friendships. If your friend leads you away from the truth, and away from the church, that is not a good friend. And if you are not leading your friends to the Lord, you are not a good friend either.

Jonathan was a prince, the son of King Saul, and was very wealthy. David was a shepherd and was poor. Jonathan took off his princely robe and put it on David, then he gave him his armor, sword, and belt. This is symbolic of true friendship. True friendship elevates and leads to equality.

David had on shepherd's clothes. He had a sling and rocks. Jonathan loved David as his own soul. He was one in spirit with David, so he took his own clothes and weapons and put David in them.

This is a great example of unselfishness in friendship. Have you ever had a selfish friend? Most of us have had a selfish friends. Maybe you are that selfish friend. A selfish friend is the kind of friend that demands that you defer to them. You have to play their games, according to their rules. You always have to do what they want to do. Parents, watch your kids closely! If you see this characteristic in your sons or daughters, correct it quickly. If your child is the one demanding that everyone do what they want to do when they want to do it and how they want to do it, correct it. Teach your

Seeking Virtue

kids to act like Jonathan. Teach them to be unselfish and to listen to their friends and be considerate.

True love is never grasping. It never says, "What can you do for me?" and "What else can you do for me?" True love is always like this: "Is there something I can do for you?" That's love. My heart, my life, my soul, my fame, my fortune, my everything is yours. First Samuel 18:4 says, "And Jonathan took off the robe that was on him and gave it to David, with his armor, even to his sword and his bow and his belt."

Jonathan was content with second place

In 1 Samuel 23:17, Jonathan said to David, "You shall be king over Israel, and I shall be next to you." If there was any man in Israel who had reason to be jealous of David, it was Prince Jonathan. He was a hero soldier, but the gallantry of David had overshadowed him. He was the heir to the throne. But, if David was to rule over Israel, Jonathan had to be removed. Jonathan knew this, and so did King Saul. David had been anointed by Samuel to be king. Either Jonathan or David had to be removed. Here we see that there is no envy in Jonathan's heart!

This is a remarkable story in light of the history of kings and kingdoms. The pages of history, including the subsequent history of Israel, are filled with stories of bloodshed between brothers who fought over the throne of their kingdoms. But Jonathan was different, and he said to David in 1 Samuel 23:17, "You will be king over Israel and I will be next to you!"

What makes this even more striking is the fact that the only reason from a worldly perspective that David was able to survive was due to the friendship of Jonathan and his willingness to step aside. Jonathan was willing to be in second place to David. It was not because he did not want to be king, nor because he thought that David was better. Jonathan saw truth in David. This is why he was willing to step aside. Jonathan was motivated by his faith. Jonathan saw years before, with his own eyes, a young shepherd boy with nothing but a sling and some rocks go out and battle a nine-foot-tall giant, who made every other man in Israel shrink in fear, including himself.

Jonathan knew why David did this: David fought Goliath because Goliath had defied the name of the true God. Jonathan knew that, in David, there was extraordinary faith. Jonathan, because he was a man of faith, knew that God chose David to be king and not him.

That is faith—a magnanimous spirit that is rare in the history of man. The humility of Jonathan is what made him great in the eyes of God. Jonathan could have asserted his worldly rights. He could have conspired and killed David and ascended to the throne. In history though, Jonathan would have been remembered as a petty king who did nothing great with his life. However, in humility, the willingness to be in second place and discern the moving of God in David's life, Jonathan is enshrined in true greatness for all eternity.

The lesson for us is abundantly clear. It is for God to raise us up in this world. We are to strive to serve him, and if his place for us is first place or if it is last, we are to be willing to walk in it. Ultimately, greatness in this world means nothing unless it is given by God. Jesus said that there are many who are first now who will be last in heaven; and there are many who are last now who will be first in heaven. In that respect, Jonathan had a genuine faith, was a true friend, was his own man, and was content to accept second place.

This world can be a lonely place without true, loyal friends. The world can be discouraging and brutal, and friendship is a thing you need. The Roman statesman Cicero wrote a book entitled "On Friendship." What follows are a few quotes from this book. Cicero said:

> Now friendship may be thus defined: a complete accord on all subjects human and divine, joined with mutual goodwill and affection.[20]

When you have a friend with whom you can share your faith and politics and be in agreement in most areas of life, you have found a treasure. You need this kind of friend: a friend who you can confide in, and with whom you can share your thoughts and convictions.

To maintain such a friendship requires that you are at peace with yourself. We have already seen what envy does to the human spirit. If you are a true friend, you will rejoice in your friend's promotion and success, as Jonathan did with David. Being a good friend to others requires that you feel good toward yourself. On that subject Cicero said,

> For when a man's confidence in himself is greatest, when he is so fortified by virtue and wisdom as to want nothing and to feel absolutely self-dependent, it is then that he is most conspicuous for seeking out and keeping up friendships.[21]

---

20. Cicero, *Letters*, 15.
21. Cicero, *Letters*, 19.

Another thing to consider about the friends you need is this: true friends will not ask you to do things that are wrong. If you have a so-called friend who wants you to compromise your faith or lie for them, this is not the kind of friendship you need. Cicero made this point when he stated,

> We may then lay down this rule of friendship—neither ask nor consent to do what is wrong. For the plea "for friendship's sake" is a discreditable one, and not to be admitted for a moment.[22]

Never fall into that trap when someone says, "I thought you were my friend." True friends speak plainly. You are not being a good friend if you do not speak the truth. Cicero stated:

> Compliance gets us friends, plain speaking hate. Plain speaking is a cause of trouble, if the result of it is resentment, which is poison of friendship; but compliance is really the cause of much more trouble, because of indulging his faults it lets a friend plunge into headlong ruin. But the man who is most to blame is he who resents plain speaking and allows flattery to egg him on to his ruin.[23]

True friends avoid gossip and slander. When one friend speaks to you in a negative way about another friend, it is always best to hold your tongue and let time sort out who is the true friend. Valerius Maximus related the following example of Plato, with his pupil Xenocrates:

> He had heard that Xenocrates had made many disrespectful remarks against him; without the slightest hesitation, Plato refused to consider this accusation. His informer kept insisting with a convincing look on his face, and he asked Plato why he didn't trust him; Plato replied that it was not believable that he should like someone so much and not be liked by him in return. Finally, the malicious fellow, who was trying to stir up trouble between friends, resorted to taking an oath. Plato did not want to argue about whether he was perjuring himself, so he declared that Xenocrates would never have said such things unless he had felt that they would be of some good to Plato. You would think that Plato's soul had spent its lifetime not in a mortal body but wearing a suit of armor in the citadel of heaven; it fought invincible and beat off all attacks by human vices, and it kept every aspect of virtue safely enclosed in its lofty embrace.[24]

---

22. Cicero, *Letters*, 22.

23. Cicero, *Letters*, 39.

24. Maximus, *Memorable Deeds and Sayings*, 126–27.

Plato gave us a superb example of true friendship. He was not willing to believe a negative report concerning a friend. Plato resolved to believe that, even if his friend leveled criticism towards him, behind his back, his friend only meant it for good.

A friend such as this must be completely at ease within himself or herself. It requires the absence of envy and self-seeking pride. Therefore, if you get mad at a friend for criticizing you, it is you who are lacking the qualities of true friendship.

SELF-RESTRAINT

> He who is slow to anger is better than the mighty, and he who rules his spirit than he who takes a city.
> (Prov 16:32)

We must consider self-restraint as a highly significant virtue. No one succeeds and progresses through life very far without the ability to show necessary restraint. Circumstances often rise when our first instinct in reaction is the wrong one. Such occasions require self-restraint. We have to develop the ability to restrain our emotions and our impulses. There are certain temptations that come into our lives that God will use to test our will.

Valarius Maximus gave an example of a well-known philosopher who was famous for his self-restraint. In the ancient world, philosophers were held in very high regard. The rich and powerful people of the world were drawn to them and wanted to be close with them, often offering them money so they could claim to be one of their disciples.

The Stoic and Cynic philosophers prided themselves on not needing the things of this world. They considered their souls to be free when they could be content with nothing except their reason. But you can imagine the temptation for them when the rich and powerful sought their friendship and offered them wealth and fame. Valarius Maximus described the restraint in the life of the philosopher Diogenes, when he was sought out by Alexander the Great:

> Alexander may have acquired the reputation of being unconquerable, but he was unable to conquer the self-restraint of Diogenes the Cynic. Alexander went up to Diogenes as he was sitting in the sun and urged Diogenes to tell him if there was anything he wanted. Diogenes happened to be sitting on the sidewalk, and

Seeking Virtue

although people called him scruffy, he was a man of strong moral character, so he said, "We can talk about other things later, but for now I would like you to stop blocking the sunlight." This was the meaning behind those words: Alexander is trying to unseat Diogenes with his riches, but it will be easier for Alexander to unseat Darius with his armies.[25]

Diogenes's self-restraint was so strong that not even the riches of Alexander impressed him. He was more interested in enjoying the sun than in entertaining the most powerful man in the world.

Christians today must show self-restraint in their emotions and reactions to stressful situations, especially in our culture of consumerism. For example, we should show restraint in our eating. Socrates once said,

> The rest of the world lived to eat, while he himself ate to live.[26]

Those who are able to master their appetites through self-restraint are better suited to be in service to the Lord. Those who are controlled by their passions and emotions are often too unstable to be trusted by the Lord.

LOVE

> Beloved let us *love* one another, for *love* is of God; and everyone who *loves* is born of God and knows God. He who does not *love* does not know God, for God is *love*.
> (1 John 4:7–8)

John says that we are to love one another, and if we do not love one another then we do not know God. Love is a characteristic of God, and if God lives within us, love is there. This godlike love is not dependent on how others treat us. We are to love even when others are not being loving. Polybius gave us an example of this higher form of love from ancient Greece:

> You should not only read tragedies, myths, and stories but know well and ponder over such things. In all of them we see that those brothers who, giving way to wrath and discord, carried their quarrel to excess, not only in every case brought destruction on themselves but utterly subverted their substance, their families and their cities; while those who studied even in moderation to

---

25. Maximus, *Memorable Deeds and Sayings*, 137.
26. Diogenes, *Lives of Eminent Philosophers*, 165.

love anyone and tolerate each other's errors, were the preservers of all these things, and lived in the greatest glory and honour.[27]

According to the experience of Polybius, those who are successful and honorable are those who learn to love others, even when they are in error. If we allow ourselves to continue in disunity with our family and friends, it will not take long for our emotions to lead us into excess. Love conquers our emotions. When we love even those who are being unlovable, we are never more godlike because God is love.

John the apostle is often called the beloved apostle because in the Gospels he is referred to as the disciple Jesus loved. He declares emphatically through the inspiration of the Holy Spirit that God is love! God reveals himself to the world through his word and through his chosen apostles. The way he chose to describe his very being is: "God is love."

There is a need in all of us to know we are loved by God and others. It is good for parents to tell their children that they love them. It is good for a husband to tell his wife, "I love you." That is the kind of love God has for us. It is like the love a parent has for their newborn child. I have four children and, with each one of them, I can remember holding them in my hands and looking at their little faces and all their delicate features and just falling in love with them. I could just sit there and stare into that little face. Then, of course, they start crying and that magical moment is over. But such love is powerful, binding, and unchanging. God loves you because he created you. He knows everything about you. Like a mother gazing at the face of her newborn child, God loves you.

But you have to be born to him, or you are not God's child. Perhaps you are reading this and have not felt the love of God in your life. You have never sensed the love of God and the gaze of God fixed on you. The reason for that may be that you are not his child, and you need to be born into God's family. That happens when you call on the name of Jesus. When you believe in Jesus, that is when you become his child.

God said in Proverbs 8:17, "I love those who love me and those who seek me diligently will find me." If you make a decision to seek after God diligently, you will find him in Jesus, and the promise of God is that he loves you.

In Hosea 11:1–4, God spoke through the prophet and said, "When Israel was a child, I loved him, and out of Egypt I called my son. . . . I drew them with gentle cords, with bands of love, and I was to them as those who

---

27. Polybius, *Histories*, Loc. 14363–67.

Seeking Virtue

take the yoke from their neck." Egypt symbolizes the world, the kingdom of Satan. We are all born into the bondage of this world. When we seek after God, he calls us out of Egypt and draws us with bands of love. But you might say, "I am a sinner, how can God love me? I have too much sin." In that respect, Hosea 14:4 says, "I will heal their backsliding, I will love them freely, for my anger has turned away from him." Similarly, Romans 5:8 states, "But God demonstrates his own love toward us, in that while we were still sinners, Christ died for us." God so loves the world—that means every person in it—that he came into this world in the person of Jesus and paid the penalty for our sins, to give us salvation for free. All he asks from us is to believe him, to trust him, and to call on his name.

You do not have to be perfect to experience God's love. Think of all the great sinners in the Bible through whom God demonstrated his love. They struggled with all the same sins which still plague us today:

- God loved David so much that, even though David committed great sexual sin, he forgave him.

- God loved Elijah so much that, even though Elijah greatly doubted his plan, God protected him.

- God loved Jonah so much that, even though he tried to run away from him, God brought him back.

- God loved Saul of Taurus so much that, though he had intense hate in his heart and persecuted Christians, God forgave him and changed his name to Paul and used him to be the greatest church planter in history.

- God loved Peter so much that, even though he denied him three times, God forgave him.

Do you struggle with sexual sin? The sin of doubt? Are you like Jonah and your sin is that you are disobeying God and running from him? Maybe you are like Saul and have hate in your heart. Maybe you have committed the sin of Peter and, to this point in your life, you have denied Christ.

God loves you and the world so much that he gave his only son as a sacrifice for sin. Jesus said in Revelation 3:19, "As many as I love, I rebuke and chasten, therefore be zealous and repent." Notice what Jesus said: be "zealous" and repent. Be zealous; stop being lukewarm; stop being callous towards God; stop being indifferent about the word of God. Step out in your faith, get "on fire" for the Lord. This can only happen if you love the Lord with all your heart.

PEACE

> Now may the Lord of *peace* Himself give you *peace* always in every way. The Lord be with you all.
> (2 Thess 3:16)

One of the most common pursuits of mankind is to find peace. However, there are so many things in this world that take away our peace, and finding it can be very difficult. All the pressures we face at work and at home, with the negativity on social media and the news, work together to create a constant state of stress and emotional fatigue. Without question what we need is peace. For the Christian, there is only one place where peace can be found: through Jesus Christ.

God is willing to share peace with you

Paul said in the passage cited above, "May the Lord of peace Himself give you peace." This reveals something very important for all peace-seekers today: God is willing to share peace with you.

Jesus said in John 14:27, "Peace, I leave with you, My peace I give to you; not as the world gives do I give to you, let not your heart be troubled, neither let it be afraid." Notice that the text says, peace is *given* to us. It is not merely offered to you, but it is a treasure that Jesus says he will "leave with you" and "give" to you. God has the power to breathe peace into the heart, to create peace in the soul. He says, "My peace I give to you." How would you like to have his peace?

Can you imagine Jesus, the Creator of the heavens and the earth, the one who knows and commands all things, having anxiety? Can you imagine him ever being confused? Jesus was always at peace, even in the garden when he sweated blood out of the anguish he felt in his soul before the crucifixion. Even in anguish, Jesus was at peace. He said, "Not my will, Father, but your will be done." Jesus was at perfect peace because he is peace; and he says, "My peace I leave with you, I give it to you." It is ours for the taking. You can either take his peace, or you can take what is yours in this world: anxiety, discontent, confusion, and stress. It is a choice that we all make every day.

There are many things in this world that we can point to that rob us of peace. It may be an unhappy marriage, worries over our children, or the stress of being so busy that there is no time to do anything. We are robbed of peace because of our discontent. However, we are wise to recognize that those struggles we all face are also the means God uses to draw us to himself. In other words, we find peace through the difficulties we are facing.

Sometimes though, when our lives are at peace for extended periods of time, and we are prosperous, it is then that we become discontent. As Tacitus described when the Roman Empire was at peace for an extended period of time,

> Peace was scarcely broken—if at all. Rome was plunged in gloom.[28]

It is not uncommon that, even when we are at peace, and all of our fears are calmed and everything is going great, gloom comes upon us. We look at our lives, and we feel we are in a rut. Those feelings of discontent rise up, and we question: "Why am I doing this?"

Sometimes, even in prosperity, we have feelings of anxiety because it all feels meaningless. The culprit who robs us of our peace is the flesh. The flesh wars against the Holy Spirit within us, and if we are not seeking the Lord and walking in the Spirit, the flesh causes us to feel the burden of sin and we become discontent. Paul said in Philippians 4:11, "I have learned in whatever state I am, to be content." That essentially means to be at peace.

Sometimes, when everything is great in our lives, discontent is strongest. We have the feeling that we are not happy, and we ask, "What's next?" "Surely there is more to life than this." Discontent makes us feel alone. But, you really are not alone. People respond to this in a number of different ways. Some people try to find peace in their hearts by trying to get more: "If I can make more money, I will have peace. If I change churches, maybe that will bring me more peace." Sadly, when we do these things and a little time goes by, those same feelings well up within us again.

Why are we empty? Because God has created us for himself. We can only find peace in him. He is willing to give us peace, but we have to go to him. Find your peace in him; rest in him.

If God wants you somewhere other than where you are, he will create the circumstances in your life to move you. God's will for your life is that

---

28. Grant, *Annals of Imperial Rome*, 173.

you stay close to him and let that be enough for you. If you are poor and need a new job, seek him, rest in him, and work for him. Let God bring peace to you where you are, and God will add to you whatever else he desires. There is nothing better for us to do than to rest in him.

Some will say, "Well, if I just do this, if I buy a new house, if I get this new job—then I will be happy." That may help for a while. However, true lasting peace is the peace that we receive from him. God is willing to share that peace with you, but it is not found by you making changes. It is found only when he gives it to you. God is willing to give you his peace.

God is able to give you peace always

The apostle Paul said in 2 Thessalonians 3:16, "Now may the Lord of peace himself give you peace always in every way." Paul says not only will he give it to you once, but always. We can have peace in every situation: in every part of the day, the morning, and the evening, when you are tired and stressed. Billy Graham wrote a book entitled *Peace with God*, in which he said:

> In the restless sea of human passions, Christ stands steadfast and calm, ready to welcome all who will turn to Him and accept the blessings of safety and peace.[29]

If you lack peace with God, Jesus is always ready to give you peace. If you lack peace at home, Jesus, the owner of peace, is always willing to give it to you. May the Lord of peace give you peace always, in every circumstance!

If you are poor, the Lord can make you rich in faith. Are you sick? The Lord always has patience to give to us; he can make you feel glory in the midst of such affliction. Peace is always available.

Isaiah described peace like a river that never runs dry. It is always flowing, but you have to go there and drink from it. The peace that the Lord offers to us does not mean exemption from trials. It also does not mean that he removes the spiritual battles from our lives. But it is a promise of peace being available through all these difficulties.

No one is immune from sorrow, but the Christian can be immune from despair. We have a river of peace flowing through us. All we have to do is drink from it. Jesus, the Lord of peace, gives peace always. Jesus said in Matthew 11:28, "Come to Me all you who labor and are heavy laden, and I will give you rest."

---

29. Graham, *Peace with God*, 16.

Seeking Virtue

God gives peace in every way

Paul said in 2 Thessalonians 3:16, may the Lord give you peace always and "in every way." God is able to bring peace into our lives in every way that can possibly be imagined. For example, he can bring you peace by bringing a bad storm into your life. He can bring peace by providing calm in your life. He can give you peace by removing your wealth. He can even bring you peace by giving you wealth. In the movie *Fiddler on the Roof*, Tevia's future son-in-law said, "Money is the world's curse." Tevia looked up to heaven and said "Yes, and may the Lord smite me with it!"

God can bring peace into your life through sickness, even through death. In Christ, peace is available through every circumstance life may bring. The Lord knows that you desire peace, and he can bring peace into your life. It will be tailor-made just for you.

Peace is dependent on God

This peace that comes from God is entirely dependent upon him. Isaiah 26:3–4 says, "You will keep him in perfect peace, whose mind is stayed on You, because he trusts in You. Trust in the Lord forever, for in Yah, the Lord, is everlasting strength." God is the one who can give perfect peace and keep us in perfect peace. If you desire peace, learn from God's word that your peace is also dependent on God keeping it for you. The text in the original is "you will keep him in peace, peace." It is the Hebraic way of expressing the idea of peace emphatically: true and real peace; double peace; peace of great depth and vast extent.

This is a spiritual peace that is only available to those who are spiritually born again. Jesus said, "Where your treasure is, there your heart will be also" (Matt 6:21). Therefore, if all your treasure is in this world, that is where your heart will be. If this world is your true residence, you are going to be subjected to all the things that go with living in this world.

Think about all the things in this world that rob us of peace. We deal with fear: fear of losing our money and jobs; fear of terrorists; fear of a corrupt government; fear of our justice system being politicized in support of one political group over another. This is a fearful thing, especially for those who count this world their home.

In this world, fear is the price to be paid for taking up residence here. If your peace is dependent on good health, or a stable economy, or on politicians, or worldly entertainment, you need to face the truth that this world does not produce peace. Peace is dependent upon God. Not only peace, but perfect peace. With our spiritual citizenship being in heaven, our place in this world does not need to be secure. This world is not our home; our address is secure in another city that is not of this world.

Who is he that can harm you, if you are reconciled to God? The Scripture says in Romans 8:31–33, "If God be for us, who can be against us? . . . Who shall lay anything to the charge of God's elect?" If we are spiritually living in God's city, our peace is no longer tied to the things of this world, and the result is perfect peace.

Psalm 112:1, 7 says, "Blessed is the man who fears the Lord, who delights greatly in His commandments. . . . He will not be afraid of evil tidings; his heart is steadfast, trusting in the Lord, his heart is established, he will not be afraid." God keeps us in peace because we look to him, not to the circumstances of this world. Our security is in him; our hope is in him. Jeremiah 29:11 says, "For I know the thoughts that I think toward you, says the Lord, thoughts of peace and not of evil, to give you a future and a hope." God has created a city of peace for his children, and he has thoughts of peace for those who belong to him.

Perhaps you have read this and though you are a Christian, you still do not have peace. Thus, you question, "Why do I not have peace?" "I am filled with anxiety, I am stressed out. I have no peace." "I have asked God for peace but I have not received it."

The truthful answer to this question is: the lack of peace in most Christians is attributed to some secret cause. We must remove all the secret sins that are robbing us of peace. Too many Christians try to live in two cities rather than just choosing one. They have an address in heaven, but they also have an address in this world, and they are trying to straddle the two. The Scripture says in James 1:8, "The double-minded man is unstable in all of his ways." For many of us, this is why we do not have peace: we are doubleminded.

If you desire perfect peace, you must surrender to the Lord. When you do that, Paul says in Philippians 4:7, "The peace of God, which passes all understanding, shall keep your hearts and minds through Christ Jesus."

Seeking Virtue

Peace is dependent on a focused mind

Isaiah 26:3 says, "You will keep him in perfect peace, whose mind is stayed on you." To "stay" our mind on God means to "fix" our mind on him, to count on him, to depend on him, to be focused on him.

What is your mind stayed on? Some fix their minds on friends. Some are focused upon their own abilities, or on their children or spouse; but peace will only come to those whose minds are focused on God. To have your mind *stayed* on God means to put all your confidence in him. As Christians, our minds need to be focused on Christ. We need each other to be focused.

I love being around people who are focused on Christ. They are not easily shaken or deceived. They are not easily swayed by gossip or rumors. They are grounded and settled in God's truth, and they are peaceful.

The lives of most people are driven by trying to keep the things they want in this world. As a result, they are slaves to this world. It will not be until they give up those things to God and focus on him that they will experience the peace that God promises us. This is a truth that even the ancient philosophers grasped. The Stoic philosophers of the Roman Empire possessed an enlightened view of the world and providentially helped prepare the world for the message of the church. Epictetus, who wrote a history of Stoic philosophy said to his followers:

> Give up wanting to remain in Corinth, and, in a word, give up wanting anything but what God wants. And who will prevent you, who will compel you? No one, any more than anyone prevents or compels Zeus. When you have such a leader as Zeus and identify your wishes and your desires with His, why are you still afraid that you will fail? Give to poverty and to wealth your aversion and your desire: you will fail to get what you wish, and you will fall into what you would avoid. Give them to health; you will come to grief; so also if you give them to offices, honours, country, friends, children, in short to anything that lies outside the domain of moral purpose. But give them to Zeus and the other gods; entrust them to their keeping, let them exercise the control; let your desire and your aversion be ranged on their side—and how can you be troubled any longer?[30]

This is sage advice, even if it is from a pagan poet. Those old stoics may have been influenced by the prophets of Israel. For example, Isaiah said

---

30. Epictetus, *Discourses*, 1:335.

stay your mind on God and you will find perfect peace. Also, David said in Psalm 112:7 that such a man or woman "will not be afraid of evil tidings; his heart is steadfast, trusting in the Lord."

It is not easy to focus our minds on God when almost everything around us that we see and hear is pulling on us and tempting us. We have to train ourselves to focus on the Lord. That is why we are connected together in church families: to exhort each other, to cheer each other on, to encourage each other when we fail, and to pray for each other. We have to learn to fix our minds on God. Alexander Maclaren said in one of his sermons,

> If a man holds out to God a tremulous hand with a shaking cup in it, which he sometimes presents and sometimes twitches back, it is not to be expected that God will pour the treasure of His grace into such a vessel, with the risk of most of it being spilt upon the ground. There must be a steadfast waiting if there is to be a continual flow.[31]

God keeps us in perfect peace when our mind is focused on him. As Paul said in Philippians 4:6–7, "Be anxious for nothing, but in everything by prayer and supplication, with thanksgiving, let your requests be made known to God; and the peace of God, which surpasses all understanding will guard your hearts and minds through Christ Jesus."

Peace is dependent on trusting God

Isaiah said that God will keep the believer in perfect peace when his mind is stayed in him, "because he trusts in him." Isaiah continued, "Trust in the Lord forever, for Yah, the Lord, is everlasting strength" (Isa 26:4). Here we see that peace is dependent on trusting the Lord, putting our faith into his promises to us. If we trust him to give us peace, he will be faithful to give it to us. No matter what you are struggling with, or what you are fearing, trust in him. Nothing is too big for him, or too complicated. It is impossible for you to have messed up so badly that he cannot intervene and change your circumstances. Only trust in him!

One of our children is a girl adopted from China, and adoption is very important to us. Several years ago my wife, Dana, and I participated in a fundraiser to raise awareness for adoption. The fundraiser was centered on

---

31. Maclaren, "The Inhabitant of the Rock," in Maclaren, *Expositions of Holy Scripture*, n.p.

people donating funds to see us rappel down a skyscraper in downtown Baton Rouge. They asked us to do it six months in advance, and I said yes.

But as that day approached, I was dreading what I committed to do. As we rode up the elevator to the top of this skyscraper, I was terrified. They hooked me up to a rig for rappelling, led me to the edge of the building, and told me to lean back. I stood on the top of that building, the Mississippi River roaring below me. I did not look at anything, I just wanted down! I had to lean back and put all my trust in that rig; I had to trust that they had hooked me up correctly. I leaned back in blind trust. Now, I had no peace, *until my feet hit the ground.*

In the same way we have to trust God. We must put all of our weight onto him and let him hold us up. Sooner or later, our feet will hit the ground. Perfect peace will come over us, but we have to trust him first.

Isaiah says, "Trust in the Lord forever." The word "forever" in the prophetical books is a figure for "always" or "continuously." Even in times when trust seems to have no foundation, we may keep on trusting, because our trust is in God. This is a call to put our faith in him, the one who is always faithful, to build your life on the Rock of Ages.

Our faith and trust must be in him alone, for nothing else will bring peace. We cannot put our trust in things, because the things of this world pass away. We cannot put our trust in man, because all of us know that even our friends sometimes are the cause of our most bitter disappointments. We cannot put our trust in our own selves, because we know our own weaknesses and fears.

If we are seeking perfect peace, we must put our trust in God and in him alone. He is an "everlasting Rock." He has been abundantly proven. Secure and blessed always are they who put their trust in him.

Polybius, the ancient Roman historian, described the practice of the Roman legions that they called "to the faith." When their legions defeated an enemy on the battlefield, or after they had laid siege to a rebellious city and the inhabitants of the city finally surrendered, they were required to surrender "to the faith." To surrender "to the faith" meant that there were no terms. For those who surrendered "to the faith," they had no right to make any demands. They were conquered and at the mercy of the conqueror.[32]

We need to surrender "to the faith." We "have peace with God through our Lord Jesus Christ"; but we also have to surrender "to the faith." We were enemies of Christ, but we are conquered. Do not try to make deals

---

32. Polybius, *Histories*, Loc. 13091–96.

with Christ. Do not try to draw up terms. Just surrender! When Jesus is our conqueror we must lay down all those things that were keeping us from him. When we surrender in faith to him, Jesus gives us peace.

Be a peacemaker

Not only are we called by God to live in peace, but we are to be peacemakers. In the Sermon on the Mount, Jesus said in Matthew 5:9, "Blessed are the peacemakers." Too many who identify themselves as Christians are troublemakers rather than peacemakers. If you are constantly in a state of discontent, if you find fulfillment when you hear rumors and backbiting, if you are always finding fault with others and being negative, it is quite possible that you are not a Christian.

Jesus Christ entered into this world with the title "Prince of Peace," and those who follow him should evidence the same peacemaking spirit as their Lord. Unfortunately, being a peacemaker has different meanings for different people.

It is vital that we understand what it means to be a peacemaker according to God's word and not according to any man-made assumptions. A peacemaker is not the kind of person who does not care what anyone else does as long as it does not directly affect him or her. That is how some think: "Well I do not want to insert myself into anyone else's life."

Some think being a peacemaker means tolerance. They say, "You do your thing and I'll do mine; what is right for you might not be right for me." This is not the Spirit of Christ. Jesus told the woman caught in adultery, "Go and sin no more" (John 8:11). He forgave her, but he did not endorse her sexual sin.

Some think a peacemaking means appeasement or peace at any price. Appeasement does not make for peace. It just delays the conflict. The history of Europe during the 1930s is the classic example of this. Churchill, commenting on the liberal disarmament movement before the Second World War, said,

> Virtuous motives, trammeled by inertia and timidity, are no match for armed and resolute wickedness. A sincere love of peace is no excuse for muddling hundreds of millions of humble folk into total war. The cheers of weak, well-meaning assemblies soon cease to echo, and their votes soon cease to count. Doom marches on.[33]

33. Churchill, "Gathering Storm," 190.

The appeasers in the British government labeled Churchill a warmonger and a hater. But it was the appeasers of Hitler that allowed him to rearm Germany. And history tells us what happened: millions died. The great preacher Alexander Maclaren said:

> And there are people who love peace, and seek after it in the cowardly fashion of letting things alone; whose "peace-making" has no nobler source than hatred of trouble, and a wish to let sleeping dogs lie. These, instead of being peacemakers, are war-makers, for they are laying up materials for a tremendous explosion some day.[34]

If your understanding of peacemaking is appeasement, tolerance, or avoidance of all conflict, instead of peacemaking, you are actually producing more conflict.

So what is a blessed peacemaker? A peacemaker is above all a person of honesty. A peacemaker does not say all is well when it actually is not. If there is a problem, he or she readily admits it. God, through the prophet Ezekiel, warned against those who act as if all is well when it is not, "who say 'Peace,' when there is no peace" (Ezek 13:10). God said that people who do this are not peacemakers but are seducers and liars. Instead, the peacemaker is painfully honest about the true status of relationships in the world, and honest in his or her own personal dealings. The peacemaker admits failed relationships and does not avoid conflict in hopes that it will go away.

Think about how important this is in the home. If the husband is not a peacemaker, but a conflict avoider, he will not talk about his true feelings with his wife and he will hold on to hurts and offenses. Such behavior never brings peace into the home. In fact, it does the opposite: it is just a matter of time before those stored-up hurt feelings come pouring out in anger.
The peacemaker refuses to say, "Peace, peace!" when there is no peace. A peacemaker is a person of honesty.

A peacemaker is also willing to be rejected for the sake of true peace. Anytime we try to deal honestly with real sin and real division, it brings with it the risk of being rejected. This is why we are tempted to avoid true peacemaking altogether. It is easy to rationalize that trying to bring true peace will "only make things worse."

Jesus is the Prince of Peace. But Jesus also said in this world his truth would cause division, and son will turn against father, and brother against brother. Why does the peace of Jesus Christ sometimes cause division?

---

34. Maclaren, *Beatitudes and other Sermons*, 64.

Because the peace that Christ offers requires submission and change. If a person does not want to change, or if they do not want to submit to the lordship of Christ, it causes division. In this world the flesh wars against the spirit.

Someone once said that "the peacemaker is a fighter." A peacemaker sometimes must make trouble to make peace, but they strive to do so in a winsome way. Paul said in Romans 14:19, "Make every effort to do what leads to peace and to mutual edification." And in 12:18 of the same book Paul said, "If it is possible, as far as it depends on you, live at peace with everyone." Notice that Paul said, "*if* it is possible." If peace requires us to sacrifice the truth; if peace requires us to compromise; to roll over; to be wrongly tolerant; then there is no true peace.

Chapter 6

Live with an Eternal Perspective

The appearance of the wheels and their workings was like the color of beryl, and all four had the same likeness. The appearance of their workings was, as it were, a wheel in the middle of a wheel.

(EZEKIEL 1:16)

The wheels of Ezekiel symbolize the working providence of God. God is always working in the lives of his children: any way we turn, in any choice we make, God's wheels of providence propel us to his chosen destination for us. Herodotus stated in his great work of history,

> But if thou feelest thyself to be a man, and a ruler of men, lay this first to heart, that there is a wheel on which the affairs of men revolve, and that its movement forbids the same man to be always fortunate.[1]

This is the experience of all mankind. We fight our battles and work hard. We prepare for a long life and save for retirement. We live our life with insecurity in the hope that, one day, we will arrive to the point where we can retire and just enjoy life.

But that is a delusion, because just when we arrive at that place when we think we can kick back and enjoy our own little kingdom that we have

---

1. Herodotus, *Histories*, 92.

spent our lives building, we realize we could lose it all. We have that vision that pops into our thoughts, reminding us life is not forever. "What happens after I die?" Fear grips our souls, and we find that we still do not have the peace and security we expected.

At one point in time or another, you will be confronted by the harsh reality that you are merely a created being, and that there is a spiritual part of you that will live on after you die in this world. Jesus said that those who never think about eternity are fools. In fact, he gave a parable that specifically focused on a rich businessman who had worked his whole life saving up money. He saved and saved, until finally he said to himself, "I have all I need, now it is time to eat, drink and be merry."

Jesus said such a person is a fool: "This night your soul will be required of you" (Luke 12:20). All that money you saved, and all that stuff for which you worked so hard, will be enjoyed by some other person.

LIFE IS SHORT

> Whereas you do not know what will happen tomorrow. For what is your life? It is even a vapor that appears for a little time and then vanishes away.
> (Jas 4:14)

Marcus Aurelius once stated:

> Since it is possible that thou mayest depart from life this very moment, regulate every act and thought accordingly.[2]

Very similarly James 4:14 says your life is "a vapor that appears for a little time and then vanishes away." Some may read that verse and think, "That is a depressing verse. I do not want to think about my life being over quickly. In fact, I will spend my days filling them with so much activity that I will not think about it." By contrast, God's word teaches us that life is short and, to live the Christian life in a healthy way, we need to constantly live like we are dying. We need to live with the end in mind.

Otherwise, we are just like the world and no different than unbelievers. To the world, this life is all there is. It is all they desire. But for Christians, we are only pilgrims in this world. Thus, it is a mark of wisdom to live as if you are dying.

---

2. Aurelius, *Meditations*, Loc. 219–20.

It is only when we realize the brevity of life that our present choices and actions will be carefully weighed.

We tend to forget about how short life is. We fool ourselves into thinking that this little sin does not matter. Or we think we can live it up now and that religion can come later. In James 4:14 the brother of the Lord warned, "You do not know what will happen tomorrow." And then he added this powerful question, "for what is your life?" James answered the question by comparing our life to a vapor that is here one moment and gone the next.

The shortness of life is a common theme throughout the Bible. In Job 25:9, Job bitterly complained, "Now my days are swifter than a runner." The word for "runner" can also be translated "post." He was referring to the ancient equivalent of a post office. Swift horses would be stationed along the postal route a certain number of miles apart, and the runner would ride a horse until it was tired and then would jump on the second, and so on from there.

In our day and time, with email, cell phones, and overnight delivery, the ancient postal service is not too impressive. But in the ancient world, nothing was faster. This is a good illustration of our lives that Job uses. Our lives are much like an ancient post office. Every year is like a swift horse: we jump on it and ride it as fast as we can and when it gets worn out and tired, the next year is waiting on us. When it is gone, we jump on the next horse. Job said that his life is like a post. It is not like a slow wagon train that drudges along. It is like a swift post.

In this same passage, Job stated, "My days are passed away as the swift ships." We would say it is like a jet airplane. Job also said that life is "as the eagle swooping on its prey." The eagle is a bird noted for its swiftness. Such is our life: it is swiftly moving to its end. Death seeks the body as its prey. We live our lives attempting to avoid death, but death is too swift to be outrun. It is like an eagle overtaking its prey.

Even if the Lord grants you a long life full of years, what is that in light of eternity? A few generations after we are gone, most likely no one will remember anything we ever did. Methuselah lived almost a thousand years on this earth and the only reason we know him at all is because his name is recorded in God's word. Had that not happened, we would know nothing of him, even though he was here for almost a thousand years.

The only one who remembers us is God. Take all the names recorded in the history books of this world and, together, they amount to a miniscule percentage of mankind. For all the rest of us, whose names never

Live with an Eternal Perspective

make their way into a history book, we are forgotten by the world... but not by God.

God has a "history book" as well. In it is recorded not only our names, but everything we ever do in this world. Our time in the world is nothing, but what we do is of eternal consequence. What is your life? Henry Thoreau wrote, "Life is a stroll upon the beach." That is about what it amounts to in the light of eternity. Similarly, Job said our life is like "sparks that fly upward." A spark is a flicker of light that immediately disappears.

A few years ago, I was on a campout with dads and sons from our church. The leader of the group asked me to give a devotional to the boys. All of these young boys had their lives entirely ahead of them, and the last thing on their little minds was the end of life. As I was speaking by the camp fire, I saw those sparks from the fire shooting up into the air, one after another. They lit up and just as quickly, they burned out. So, I told those boys, "Look at these sparks; some of them light up and shoot up and they burn out after just a few feet. Some of the others light up and they shoot up really high, but they all just last a few seconds. Boys, that is how your life is going to be. This is your chance to make good choices and live your life for the Lord."

Isaiah said that life is like a flower that fades and like the grass that withers. What is your life? It is like a vapor and just like that it is gone. In the big picture, no one but God knows the significance of your life.

God's word warns us against worldly presumption: about making decisions and counting on things that are outside of our control. Tomorrow is controlled by God. There is nothing wrong with looking to the future and making plans, but we should never do so without expressing or acknowledging our total dependence on God. We need to guard against boasting and worldly presumption, because life is uncertain. And no amount of wealth or power can deliver you from the ultimate uncertainty of life.

The greatest spiritual incentive to repenting and giving up the love of the world is the fact that life is short and there is no promise of tomorrow. When we live today doing whatever we want—forsaking God and living in sin—it is arrogant. God says in James that "all such boasting is evil" (James 4:16). We put off getting right with God, thinking that we can do it later and saying in our hearts, "God will forgive me."

In his history, Herodotus recounted a conversation between the Persian king Xerxes and his top general, Artabanos, during the Persian invasion of Greece. Xerxes had assembled the greatest army and navy the world had ever seen. All of the Greeks combined did not stand a chance on paper against the Persians. But Artabanos possessed a wisdom that Xerxes was completely lacking. Xerxes saw that his general was in anxiety, and he questioned what was bothering him:

> "I am still quite out of my mind with fear as I consider many things, but especially as I foresee that you will have to fight against two of the most formidable adversaries of all."
>
> Xerxes said, "What in the world has gotten into you? What can you mean when you say that? You think I have two of the most formidable adversaries? Would you find fault with the size of my land army? Would you think the Greek army is likely to be many times larger than ours? Or will our navy prove inferior to theirs? Or both together? Well, then, if it appears to you that our forces are insufficient, another army could be mustered at once."
>
> Artabanos then answered, "Sire, anyone with an ounce of common sense could find no fault with your present army, nor with the size of your fleet. And if you gather more forces those two adversaries I mentioned would only become still more formidable. The two I am speaking of are the land and the sea. For the sea, has no harbors anywhere that are large enough to receive your fleet and guarantee the safety of your ships should a storm arise. Since there are no ample harbors, you must realize that fortune will now rule over the affairs of men instead of men ruling over their own fortunes. The land has also become your adversary, in that if no one comes forth to oppose you, the land itself will become more and more hostile to you the farther you advance and are lured into going ever farther. So what I am saying is that by taking more and more land and spending more and more time, you will generate famine. The mark of a superior man would be to feel fear as he makes his plans, considering everything that could happen to him, and yet be able to act boldly when the time for action arrives."[3]

Artabanos possessed not only wisdom, but also an eternal perspective. He knew that an earthly king, no matter how powerful, could not control fortune. Life is uncertain. As Christians, we are here for a purpose. We are to dream great dreams. We are to plan for the future. But we need to do it with fear. Not an unholy quivering kind of fear, but the biblical kind of fear, a holy fear of God.

We know that God is in control and our lives are in his hands. He has not promised us exemption from the uncertain circumstances of this world. This world is a fallen world. It is an evil world, filled with sin and

---

3. Herodotus, *Histories*, 518.

demons, where bad things happen. But through all of the uncertainty that surrounds us, we are grounded in the knowledge that God is in control and has set an end for this world. He has given us his word to direct our steps and to guide our choices and behavior. That is why it is a great sin to leave God out of our plans. Proverbs 27:1 says, "Do not boast about tomorrow, for you do not know what a day may bring forth."

Herodotus, who wrote his history in the fourth century before Christ, related the curious way the Egyptians reminded themselves of the brevity of life:

> At drinking parties of wealthy Egyptians, they always follow the end of their dinner by having a man carry around a corpse made of wood inside a coffin. The wooden corpse is crafted so as to be most realistic, both in the way it is painted and in the way it is carved, and it measures altogether one to three feet in length. As the man displays it before each of the guests, he says, "Look at this as you drink and enjoy yourself, for you will be like this when you are dead."[4]

That is much like the difference between an unbeliever and a believer in Christ. An unbeliever spends his life attempting to build up a heavenly kingdom on earth because this is as close as he or she will ever get to heaven. But, for a believer, life in this world is as close to hell as he or she will ever be. Life in this world is short. Believers are to live life in this world in the assurance that we will be rewarded in heaven.

BEAUTIFUL IN ITS TIME

> He has made everything *beautiful* in its time. Also He has put eternity in their hearts . . .
> (Eccl 3:11)

We must make the best of the present and accommodate ourselves to it: "He has made everything beautiful in his time." Therefore, even in trials, we must learn to say, "God be praised." We must wait with patience for the full discovery of that which, to us, seems devastating. We must acknowledge that we do not know what the end will be. We must judge nothing before the time because only God knows.

We are to believe that God has made all things beautiful. Everything is done well. As in creation, so in providence, and we will see it when the

---

4. Herodotus, *Histories*, 151.

end comes: that God took all of our experiences in life and he was directing them, using them to take us where he wanted us. God takes our chaotic lives and makes them beautiful.

For three years of my life, I traveled fifty miles, from Plano, Texas, to Fort Worth and back again, almost every day. There were multiple routes I could take from my house in Plano. Every day I made a choice. I would choose a route and just go, not knowing what was ahead. Road construction and accidents are daily occurrences, and I never knew what was around the next corner. It might take one hour to get there or three, depending on the circumstances. Many times, I suffered stressful trips because unfortunate circumstances caused me to be late.

However, I soon learned that there was a better way to travel. I could turn on the radio and listen to the "traffic on the eights" on the news radio. This was before the invention of Google Maps. Every ten minutes, people in helicopters briefed drivers on the hot spots to avoid. By listening to the eye in the sky, I knew which routes were blocked and had insight into which direction to go.

After learning about the availability of traffic reports, it would have been foolish for me to continue randomly picking out a route and hoping for the best. However, this is exactly what we are tempted to do in our spiritual life. We know God wants to direct us. We know his word is a light unto our path. We know he is the one keeping life going. However, most continue living life under the sun, trusting blind luck, and then they are angry when things do not go their way. All the while, God is there ready and willing to direct them. We must change our perspective to an eternal one, and, when we do, God makes everything beautiful.

LIVE LIKE YOU ARE DYING

If we are going to live with an eternal perspective, we must learn to live like we are dying. How would we live if we knew we only had a year to live? How would our choices be different?

Such questions are part of the human experience. We all know that our time to die will come. However, it is far better for us to contemplate our demise earlier rather than later. The earlier we convince ourselves that we are not indestructible, the longer opportunity we will have to reap the benefits of making good choices. Pliny received a life-changing revelation after one of his friends was near death in sickness:

> The lingering disorder of a friend of mine gave me occasion lately to reflect that we are never so good as when oppressed with illness. Where is the sick man who is either solicited by avarice or inflamed with lust? At such a season he is neither a slave of love nor the fool of ambition; wealth he utterly disregards, and is content with ever so small a portion of it, as being upon the point of leaving even that little. It is then he recollects there are gods, and that he himself is but a man: no mortal is then the object of his envy, his admiration, or his contempt; and the tales of slander neither raise his attention nor feed his curiosity: his dreams are only of baths and fountains. These are the supreme objects of his cares and wishes, while he resolves, if he should recover, to pass the remainder of his days in ease and tranquility, that is, to live innocently and happily. I may therefore lay down to you and myself a short rule, which the philosophers have endeavoured to inculcate at the expense of many words, and even many volumes; that "we should try and realise in health those resolutions we form in sickness." Farewell.[5]

If we lived in our time of good health as we would live if we were sick and about to die, our lives would be pure. Our choices would be made in light of eternity. We would right every wrong and seek peace with God. This is the essence of living with an eternal perspective:

> I shall pass through this world but once. Any good thing, therefore, that I can do or any kindness that I can show any human being, let me do it now. Let me not defer nor neglect it for I shall not pass this way again.[6]

These lines are attributed to an American Quaker of the early nineteenth century, Stephen Grellet. Edward, the former king of England, memorized them when he was very young. He said they often influenced his actions in later life. We would be wise to let them influence ours.

WHAT YOU REALLY OWN

What in this world is really ours? If it is true that none of our material possessions will travel with us after we die, what do you really own? The ancient pharaohs were buried with their treasure, but was it really theirs?

---

5. Pliny, *Letters of Pliny*, 326.
6. Edward, *A King's Story*, 27.

No. All their stuff is still here, as decorations for museums. So, what do we really own? Epictetus gave an interesting answer:

> If all this is true and we are not silly nor merely playing a part when we say, "Man's good and man's evil lies in moral choice, and all other things are nothing to us," why are we still distressed and afraid? Over the things that we seriously care for no one has authority; and the things over which other men have authority do not concern us. What kind of thing have we left to discuss?—"Nay, give me directions."—What directions shall I give you? Has not Zeus given you directions? Has he not given you that which is your own, unhindered and unrestrained, while that which is not your own is subject to hindrance and restraint? What directions, then, did you bring with you when you came from him into this world, what kind of an order? Guard by every means that which is your own, but do not grasp at that which is another's. Your faithfulness is your own, your self-respect is your own; who, then, can take these things from you? Who but yourself will prevent you from using them? But you, how do you act? When you seek earnestly that which is not your own, you lose that which is your own.[7]

The only thing we truly own in this world, according to Epictetus, is our "moral choice." And since nothing else belongs to us, why should we worry about things that are not really ours? The things we do not really own are our material possessions: our cars, clothes, homes, and a host of other things.

All these things belong to the world. They may be ours to use while we live. But when we die, the ownership returns to the world. If that is the case, why should we worry about them now?

The world has authority over these things. However, the things that we have authority over, no man can take, and they will go with us to heaven. These things include our faithfulness, our self-respect, the thoughts of our hearts, and the words that we speak. These are the things we own and we need to treasure them more than any of the material things that are temporarily in our possession. If you spend your life seeking after things that are not your own, you will lose the things that are truly yours. We need to live with an eternal perspective.

---

7. Epictetus, *Discourses*, 1:155.

THE RACE OF LIFE

> Let us lay aside every weight, and the sin which so easily ensnares us, and let us run with endurance the *race* that is set before us, looking unto Jesus the author and finisher of our faith.
> (Heb 12:1-2)

When we live with an eternal perspective, we will not view the things of this world as prizes to be obtained. The type of house we have, or the type of car, will no longer capture our attention, because our hearts and minds are set on a bigger prize. We are living for eternity, for the reward that God has awaiting us in heaven.

In view of eternity, this life that we are living is best viewed as a race. We are temporarily in this world to live for Christ and spread the truth of the gospel. We are put in our place by God and, when we are saved, the starting gun sounds and the race begins. From that point forward, we are on a journey to heaven and we are to press on toward that goal.

The writer of Hebrews said, "Let us run with endurance the race that is set before us." When you enter into a relationship with Christ, your race is set. That means the end of your race is set as well! That finish line is just down the road, waiting to be crossed.

The Scripture tells us that it is appointed unto man to die once, and after that the judgment. The race is set, the finish line is ahead. After you cross the finish line, you will either be a winner or a loser. The key phrase in this text is "let us run." If you are not a Christian, the writer of Hebrews is effectively saying, "Get in the race!" In order to win any race, you have to be an entered contestant. You enter the race by trusting Jesus Christ as your Lord and Savior.

If you are a Christian, the writer of Hebrews says to "run with endurance." In other words, do not give up. Do not stop running. Why are there so many Christians who are not competing in the race that God has set before them? It is because something has tripped them up. The writer of Hebrews exhorts, "Let us lay aside every weight, and the sin which so easily ensnares us." These are the hinderances that keep us from running as we should.

Sadly there are many Christians who are entered into the race, but they are not running. They are on the track, but they are standing still. Others are merely jogging. Some are walking slowly with their arms dragging. Some are sitting or lying down.

Many Christians enter into the race and, out of the box, they are on a dead sprint. They are leading the race and everything is going great. Then, all of a sudden, the circumstances of life begin to trip them up. Satan throws something onto the track: they lose their job; someone at church does something that offends them and they stop running. They stop going to church, stop praying, and stop reading their Bible. It is tragic but some do not finish the race running. Time is called and the race is over for them.

The writer of Hebrews says to run the race "with endurance." In other words, we are to run with steady determination. We are to keep on keeping on even when our bodies cry out to stop. The Christian race is a marathon, not a sprint. We do not need short distance sprinters in the church. We need marathon runners, those who keep on persevering through the trials of life.

There will be trials and opposition. In fact, the Greek word for "race" is *agon* from which we get our word "agony." The race we are on is demanding and agonizing. It requires self-discipline, determination, and a will to win. If you are getting tired or frustrated, or if someone or something is tempting you to stop running, the writer of Hebrews says, "Look to those who have gone before you for encouragement." He says, "Since we have so great a cloud of witnesses." This refers to the heroes of the faith. Hebrews 11 is known as the "hall of faith" because it describes the great men and women of faith who have gone before us. Together, they become a cloud of witnesses.

If you are getting tired, keep on going like Abel; keep on being faithful like Abraham; keep on being obedient like Sarah; keep on persevering like the patriarchs Isaac, Jacob, and Joseph. Keep on overcoming affliction like Moses. There is nothing you face in life that was not experienced by these men and women of faith.

Perhaps you have seen the movie *Chariots of Fire*. It was based on a true story of a group of British Olympians, many of whom attended Cambridge. The class on which the story was based started at Cambridge in 1919, the year after the end of the First World War.

Perhaps you remember the scene of the freshman dinner where all the new students were gathered around the tables. Above the tables was a huge plaque with hundreds of names of Cambridge students who died in the war. An entire class was killed, and the master of the college made this speech:

Live with an Eternal Perspective

I take the war list and I run down it, name after name which I cannot read and which we who are older than you cannot hear without emotion, names which will be only names to you, the new college, but which to us names which summon up face after face; full of honesty, and goodness; zeal and vigor and intellectual promise, the flower of a generation, the glory of England and they died for England and all that England stands for, and now by tragic necessity their dreams have become yours, let me exhort you, examine yourselves, let each of you discover where your true chance of greatness lies, for their sakes, for the sake of your college and your country, seize this chance, rejoice in it, and let no power or persuasion deter you in your task.

This moving speech speaks to us as Christians, as we view the race set before us. Many people do not know that the main character in the movie, Eric Liddell, a gold medalist, died as a missionary in China.

When preparing for the Olympics Liddell said, "I believe God made me for a purpose for China, but He also made me fast. When I run I feel his pleasure, to give that up would be to hold him in contempt, to win is to honor Him."[8]

I exhort you to run your race and *win*. How? We win when we finish the race. We can experience the same satisfaction the apostle Paul did as he neared the finish line of his race: "I have fought the good fight, I have finished the race, I have kept the faith. Finally, there is laid up for me the crown of righteousness, which the Lord, the righteous Judge, will give to me on that Day, and not to me only but also to all who have loved His appearing" (2 Tim 4:7–8).

---

8. Boa, *Conformed to His Image*, 249.

Conclusion

There are over one hundred and sixty quotes and stories in this book. Most of them come from ancient primary sources. It is my hope and prayer that anyone who reads this book will find them inspirational and an aid to their Christian faith. The primary source of inspiration for the Christian is the Bible. There is nothing in this world, no wisdom of man, that is worthy to be held in the same esteem as God's inspired word. The wisdom of man is only helpful if it contains precepts and principles that will help propel Christians in their faith.

Even though many of the people quoted in this book are what we would call pagans, their words should not be shunned. Not even Moses shunned the advice of his pagan father-in-law, Jethro. In this regard, we can consider the advice of Erasmus, the great Humanist scholar during the Renaissance, in his *Handbook of the Christian Soldier*:

> It would be profitable to have a taste of all pagan literature, if, as I said, it is done at the appropriate time and with moderation, with caution and discrimination, as well as in a cursory manner, more in the manner of a foreign visitor than a resident, and lastly and most important, it all be related to Christ.[1]

It is in the spirit of Erasmus that this book and its contents are offered. It has been my desire to relate all these words of wisdom to Christ. In fact, over the years many of these quotes and stories have been used in my sermons to illustrate the true wisdom of God's word. It is my prayer that God will use this effort to inspire more true Christian soldiers.

---

1. Erasmus, "Handbook of the Christian Soldier," in Erasmus, *Collected Works*, 33.

Bibliography

Ambrose, Stephen E. *D-Day: June 6, 1944; The climactic battle of World War II*. New York: Simon & Schuster, 1994.
Arrian. *The Landmark Arrian: The Campaigns of Alexander*. Edited by James Romm, translated by Pamela Mensch. New York: Pantheon, 2010.
Aurelius, Marcus. *Meditations*. Translated by George Long. Kindle ed. Digireads.com, 2015.
Boa, Kenneth. *Conformed to His Image: Biblical and Practical Approaches to Spiritual Formation*. Grand Rapids: Zondervan, 2001.
Bradlee, Ben, Jr. *The Kid: The Immortal Life of Ted Williams*. New York: Little, Brown and Company, 2013.
Chernow, Ron. *Alexander Hamilton*. New York: Penguin, 2004.
Churchill, Winston S. "The Gathering Storm." Vol. 1 of *The Second World War*. Boston: Houghton Mifflin, 1948.
———. "The Grand Alliance." Vol. 3 of *The Second World War*. Boston: Houghton Mifflin, 1951.
———. "The Hinge of Fate." Vol. 4 of *The Second World War*. Boston: Houghton Mifflin, 1950.
Cicero, Marcus Tullius. *Letters of Marcus Tullius Cicero: With His Treatises on Friendship and Old Age; Letters of Gaius Plinius Caecilius Secundus*. Harvard Classics. Edited by Charles W. Eliot, translated by E. S. Shuckburgh and William Melmoth. New York: P. F. Collier & Son, 1909.
Criswell, W. A. "The Rich Man and God." https://wacriswell.com/sermons/1992/the-rich-man-and-god/.
Digby, William. "Journal, July 24–October 13, 1777." In *The American Revolution: Writings from the War of Independence*. Edited by John Rhodehamel, 306–33. New York: Library of America, 2001.
Diogenes Laertius. *Lives of Eminent Philosophers, Vol. I: Books 1–5*. Loeb Classical Library 184. Translated by R. D. Hicks. Cambridge: Harvard University Press, 1972.
Durant, Will. "Caesar and Christ." Vol. 3 of *The Story of Civilization*. New York: Simon and Schuster, 1972.
Edmondson, J. R. *The Alamo Story: From Early History to Current Conflicts*. Lanham, MD: Republic of Texas, 2001.
Edward, H. R. H. *A King's Story: The Memoirs of the Duke of Windsor*. New York: G. P. Putnam's Sons, 1951.

Bibliography

Epictetus. *The Discourses as Reported by Arrian, Vol. I: Books I–II*. Loeb Classical Library 131. Translated by W. A. Oldfather, edited by Jeffrey Henderson. Cambridge, MA: Harvard University Press, 1998.

———. *The Discourses, Vol. II: Books III–IV, Fragments, Encheiridion*. Loeb Classical Library, 218. Translated by W. A. Oldfather, edited by Jeffrey Henderson. Cambridge, MA: Harvard University Press, 1998.

Erasmus. *Collected Works of Erasmus*. Vol. 66. Edited by John W. O'Malley. Toronto: University of Toronto Press, 1988.

Estep, William R. *The Anabaptist Story: An Introduction to Sixteenth-Century Anabaptism*. Grand Rapids: William B. Eerdmans, 1996.

Franklin, Ben. *The Autobiography of Benjamin Franklin*. Edited by John Bigelow. New York: Black's Readers Service Company, 1932.

Gibbon, Edward. *The Decline and Fall of the Roman Empire*. 3 Volumes. New York: Random House, n.d.

Gilbert, Martin. *Churchill: A Life*. New York: Holt, 1991.

Goodwin, Doris Kearns. *Team of Rivals: The Political Genius of Abraham Lincoln*. New York: Simon & Schuster, 2005.

Graham, Billy. *Peace with God: The Secret of Happiness*. Nashville: W Publishing Group, 1984.

Grant, Ulysses S. *Personal Memoirs*. Edited by Caleb Carr. New York: Random House, 1999.

Hamilton, Alexander. "From Alexander Hamilton to The Royal Danish American Gazette, 6 September 1772." https://founders.archives.gov/?q=%22From%20Alexander%20Hamilton%20to%20The%20Royal%20Danish%20American%20Gazette%22&s=1111311111&r=2.

Herodotus. *The Landmark Herodotus: The Histories*. Edited by Robert B. Strassler, translated by Andrea L. Purvis. New York: Pantheon, 2007.

Maclaren, Alexander. *The Beatitudes and Other Sermons*. London: Alexander and Shepheard, 1896.

———. *Expositions of Holy Scripture*. Logos Bible Software. Grand Rapids: Baker, n.d.

Marcellinus, Ammianus. *The Roman History of Ammianus Marcellinus*. Translated by C. D. Yonge. Kindle ed. Digireads.com, 2011.

Maximus, Valerius. *Memorable Deeds and Sayings: One Thousand Tales from Ancient Rome*. Translated by Henry John Walker. Indianapolis: Hackett, 2004.

McCullough, David. *1776*. New York: Simon & Schuster, 2005.

Meacham, Jon. *Franklin and Winston: An Intimate Portrait of an Epic Friendship*. New York: Random House, 2004.

Merriam-Webster's Dictionary of Synonyms: A Dictionary of Discriminated Synonyms with Antonyms and Analogous and Contrasted Words. Springfield, MA: Merriam-Webster, 1984.

Neusner, Jacob, trans. *The Babylonian Talmud*. Vol. 1. Peabody, MA: Hendrickson, 2005.

Ovid. *Fasti*. Loeb Classical Library 253. Translated by James G. Frazier. Cambridge: Harvard University Press, 1931. https://www.theoi.com/Text/OvidFasti1.html.

Paine, Thomas. *Collected Writings*. Edited by Erick Foner. New York: Library of America, 1995.

Patrick, Symon. *The Heart's Ease: Or a Remedy against All Troubles*. London: William Pickering, 1847.

BIBLIOGRAPHY

Pliny. *Letters of Marcus Tullius Cicero: With His Treatises on Friendship and Old Age; Letters of Gaius Plinius Caecilius Secundus*. Harvard Classics. Edited by Charles W. Eliot, translated by E. S. Shuckburgh and William Melmoth. New York: P. F. Collier & Son, 1909.

Plutarch. *Plutarch's Lives: The Lives of the Noble Grecians and Romans*. 2 vols. Edited by Arthur Hugh Clough, translated by John Dryden. New York: Modern Library, 1992.

Polybius. *The Complete Histories of Polybius*. Translated by W. R. Paton. Kindle ed. Digireads.com, 2014.

Rhodehamel, John, ed. *The American Revolution: Writings from the War of Independence*. New York: Library of America, 2001.

Ségur, Philippe de. *Memoirs of an Aide-de-Camp of Napoleon 1800–1812*. Translated by H. A. Patchett-Martin. Stroud: Nonsuch, 2005.

Shakespeare, William. *Tragedy of Julius Caesar*. The Temple Shakespeare. London: Adline, 1906.

Spence, H. D. M., and Joseph S. Exell, eds. *I and II Kings*. The Pulpit Commentary 5. London: Kegan Paul, Trench & Co., 1881.

Spurgeon, Charles H. "The Pilgrim's Grateful Recollections." Sermon no. 939. https://www.ccel.org/ccel/spurgeon/sermons16.xxxii.html.

Stevenson, Robert Louis. *Selected Letters of Robert Louis Stevenson*. Edited by Ernest Mehew. New Haven: Yale University Press, 1997.

Suetonius. *The Lives of the Caesars*. Translated by John C. Rolfe. New York: Barnes & Noble, 2004.

Sunday, Billy. "The Devil's Boomerangs." In *Great Preaching on Fathers*, edited by Curtis Hutson, 223–32. Murfreesboro, TN: Sword of the Lord, 1989.

Tacitus. *The Annals of Imperial Rome*. Translated by Michael Grant. New York: Barnes & Noble, 1993.

Tuchman, Barbara. *The Guns of August*. New York: Macmillan, 1988.

Twain, Mark. *Autobiography of Mark Twain*. 3 vols. Edited by Harriet Elinor Smith. Kindle ed. Berkeley: University of California Press, 2010.

———. *The Innocents Abroad, Roughing It*. New York: Library of America, 1984.

Thucydides. *The Landmark Thucydides: A Comprehensive Guide to the Peloponnesian War*. Edited by Robert B. Strassler. Translated by Richard Crawley. New York: Free Press, 1996.

Waldo, Albigence. "Diary, December 11–29, 1777." In *The American Revolution: Writings from the War of Independence*, edited by John Rhodehamel, 400–409. New York: Library of America, 2001.

Subject Index

Achieving greatness, 58–63, 67
Adversity, 34–38, 40, 42, 47, 67–69
Avoiding burnout, 82–83
Avoiding conflict, 141–42

Boldness, 110–111

Confidence, 66
Contentment, 18, 68, 129–130
Courage, 27–28

Dangers of prosperity, 78–80, 87, 134
Diligence, 11–12, 58
Discernment, 119–121
Disloyalty, 88
Drunkenness, 103–05

Envy, 19–20, 84–85
Eternal perspective, 152, 154–55

Faith, 40–41, 139–140
Fear, 50
Flattery, 100–01
Forgiveness, 93
Fortitude, 5
Focus, 58
Friendship, 127–29

Generosity, 3–5
Genuine, 58
Good judgment, 50
Gluttony, 18, 130
Greed, 3, 21, 86

Happiness, 76
Hard work, 11–13, 58, 60, 72–76
Heart, 7, 9–10
Honesty, 26
Humility, 16–17
Hypocrisy, 101–102

Ignorance, 81–82
Integrity, 122

Judging others, 7, 122
Justice, 120–21

Kindness, 42
Knowledge, 123–24

Life is short, 145, 149–151
Love, 130–31
Lust, 94–96

Magnanimity, 15–16

Nobility, 5

Overcoming opposition, 42–44

Patience, 22
Peace, 135, 138, 141
Perseverance, 24, 68
Positive attitude, 36
Pride, 90–93
Priorities, 106–107
Providence, 37–38, 144, 148
Purity, 21

Subject Index

Respect, 25
Righteous anger, 26

Sacrifice, 65
Self-deception, 141
Self-denial, 65
Self-restraint, 129–30
Spiritual warfare, 44–45
Submission, 70
Success, 57

Taking a stand, 10

Temptation, 95–96
Tithing, 3
Tongue, 98–100
Trials, 32–38, 40

Unreasonable, 81–82

Vices, 78–80
Virtue, 2, 26–30, 84

Wisdom, 111–13, 116–18, 148

www.ingramcontent.com/pod-product-compliance
Lightning Source LLC
Chambersburg PA
CBHW051100160426
43193CB00010B/1255